CALGARY
BOOK OF
Everything

Everything you wanted to know about
Calgary and were going to ask anyway

Roberta McDonald

MACINTYRE PURCELL PUBLISHING INC.

MacIntyre Purcell Publishing Inc.
1662-#332
Lunenburg, Nova Scotia
B0J 2C0
(902) 640-3350
www.bookofeverything.com

Cover photo: Stockxpert
Photos: istockphoto: page 6, 8, 18, 34, 42, 62, 74, 92, 114, 140, 156, 170, 186
Cover and Design: Channel Communications Inc.

Printed and bound in Canada by UGS.

Library and Archives Canada Cataloguing in Publication
McDonald, Roberta
Calgary Book of Everything /
Roberta McDonald.
ISBN 978-0-9738063-5-9
Calgary (Alta.) -- Guidebooks. I. McDonald, Roberta II. Title.
FC3697.18.W35 2007   971.123'38044
2007-901783-5

Introduction

Of course no book can truly be about everything. What we hope we've done here is sketch an outline of a city that is vibrant and ever-changing. We think the *Calgary Book of Everything* gives you information about what you should know, about what you'd like to know and even information about what you didn't know you wanted to know. From the best Battle of Alberta moments, to the city's most heinous crimes, to oil patch slang, it's all here. We tell how much we earn, what we read, where we work and even what the real deal is about Stampede week.

We've explored the nooks and crannies that make Calgary the biggest small town in the land. We've written about our booming economy, our cowboy culture, our favourite restaurants and music, the First People, and the outlaws and modern day mavericks that have left their indelible mark on the city.

We believe a place is revealed through the accumulation of detail. You find it in the subtle nuances like the variations in weather or climate, its pride in its favourite sons and daughters, in the local slang, in the brutal crime and the quiet park.

We've made it our job to unearth and marshal those facts so that taken together they reveal a portrait. Calgary is a fascinating place and we truly could have filled volumes. To the pages and pages left behind, we say "next time."

An amazing team worked on this project. Kelly Inglis kept everything running smoothly. Martha Walls coordinated the research and Bruce Ramsay, Lynn MacIntyre, Carrie Anne MacIsaac, Samantha Amara, Dina O'Meara and Melanie Jones all offered their talents as researchers and writers.

Last, but certainly not least, we are greatly indebted to the amazing Calgarians who took time out of their jam-packed schedules to mine their Calgary experiences and provide us with some truly delightful top five lists. Hope you have as much fun reading this as we did putting it together.

— Roberta McDonald, August 2007

Table of Contents

Neighbours of the World

Following a national contest held in 1986, City Council adopted "Neighbours of the World" written by Barry Bowman and Tom Loney as the official song of the City of Calgary. You sense in the lyrics the optimism and spirit that capture the essence of the city, even today. A recording of the song is available from the Calgary Public Library.

This, this is the time
Here, here is the place to be
Stay, and set your spirit free
Come now, now, now, now

Let everyone know
Let everyone come to see
Our dreams turn into reality
A place for us to share

For we are neighbours of the world
A shining city we call Calgary
For we are neighbours of the world
A place for you, a place for me

A new beginning for you
Treasure all the time you spend
Calgary is your journey"s end
Come now, now, now, now

Hey, tell all the world
This, this is our finest year
You'll find your tomorrow's here
You'll find it here today

For we are neighbours of the world
A shining city we call Calgary
For we are neighbours of the world
A place for you, a place for me

Reach out, let's make a bridge
Take the hands of your brand-new friends
Share the feeling that never ends
We're neighbours of the world

Yes we are neighbours of the world
A shining city we call Calgary
For we are neighbours of the world
A place for you, a place for me

Calgary:

A Timeline

12500 Before Present: Calgary is a chilly and desolate place; 85 percent of Alberta is covered by glaciers.

11000 to 12000 Before Present: The first Albertans populate the area.

1754: On March 5th, Anthony Henday becomes the first European to visit what is now Alberta.

1787: Cartographer David Thompson, accompanied by a group of Peigan, spends the winter camped along the Bow River, becoming the first recorded European to visit the Calgary area.

1873: John and Adelaide Glenn settle in what is now Fish Creek Park, becoming the first Europeans to settle in the vicinity of Calgary.

1875: In August, the North West Mounted Police build a post on the site of the future city of Calgary. A year later the site is named Fort Calgary.

1879: George Cliff King and Louise Monroe are the first European couple to marry in Calgary.

1883: On November 19th, John Calgary Costello is the first non-Aboriginal child born in Calgary.

1883: The Canadian Pacific Railway reaches Calgary.

1883: The *Calgary Herald* begins publishing. It becomes a daily in 1885.

1884: Calgary is incorporated as a town and gets its first mayor, George Murdoch.

1886: Fire rips through Calgary's main business section, causing damage to the tune of $100,200. In the aftermath of this fire, town council passes a bylaw stipulating that all large downtown buildings be built of fire-resistant sandstone.

1887: The city's first fire hall opens at 7th Avenue.

1887: The Calgary Electric Lighting Company begins supplying power to the city.

1891: The last spike is driven on the Calgary and Edmonton Railway.

1893: In January, Calgary plays host to the first western Canadian recorded hockey game.

1893: Calgary is designated as a city.

1894: Wesley Fletcher Orr is elected the first mayor of the City of Calgary.

1897: A total of $1,248 is spent to build a bridge over the Elbow River.

1901: The first automobile winds its way through the streets of Calgary.

1903: "Sleepy Hollow," Calgary's first high school, opens.

1905: The province of Alberta is created from the Northwest Territories.

1906: Members of the Alberta legislature defeat a motion to relocate Alberta's capital from Edmonton to Calgary.

1909: The first streetcars roll through Calgary. They will be constant fixtures on city streets until 1950.

1912: The first Calgary Stampede, a two-day event, is held on September 2nd. In 1968 it becomes a ten-day celebration.

1914: Oil is discovered on the Dingman site near Calgary, sparking Alberta's first oil boom.

1914: The first Grand Trunk passenger train arrives in Calgary.

1917: Feminist and socialist Annie Gale is elected Alderman, making her the first woman in the British Empire to be elected to serve on a municipal council.

1918: The arrival of the Spanish Influenza epidemic leads to the banning of public meetings and makes face masks mandatory in public.

1920: Racism rears its head when Victoria Park residents unsuccessfully petition the City Council to remove "blacks" and make the area a whites-only district.

1921: Calgary teacher Agnes Macphail becomes the first woman elected to the House of Commons.

1922: In August, Calgary's first radio station, CFAC, hits the airwaves.

1923: The United Farmers of Alberta open the head office of the Alberta Wheat Pool, North America's first, in an attempt to stabilize wheat prices.

1923: Alberta's first oil refinery opens in Calgary.

Take 5 BRIAN BRENNAN'S TOP FIVE
SCALLYWAGS IN CALGARY HISTORY

Brian Brennan is the author of six bestselling books about the colourful personalities of Alberta's past. His most popular title, *Scoundrels and Scallywags: Characters from Alberta's Past*, was published by Fifth House Ltd. in 2002. To date, it has sold more than 10,000 copies.

1. **Guy Weadick.** The cowboy showman who organized the first Calgary Stampede in 1912 and in the process created one of Canada's major summer tourist attractions. Fired by the Stampede board for drinking on the job, he sued for unlawful dismissal and won. He convinced the judge that drinking was part of his job description as Stampede promoter.

2. **John Kushner.** A Calgary alderman who became legendary in media circles for his malapropisms and fractured syntax. A few typical gems from the Book of Kushner:
— I don't want the information, I just want the facts.
— It's high time we upgraded grade one to kindergarten level.
— I want to hear from the expertise.
— I'm not talking about businessmen, I'm talking about people.
— Well, don't get your dandruff up.

3. **Caroline "Mother" Fulham.** An illiterate keeper of pigs and cattle who frequently got drunk and disorderly and settled disputes with her fists. When a CPR train killed her cow after it wandered

1927: Calgary school principal William Aberhart builds his Bible college, the Prophetic Bible Institute.

1929: Calgary gets its first escalator when the T. Eaton Co. store opens at 8th Ave and 4th St.

1930: Calgary lawyer R.B. Bennett is elected Prime Minister of Canada.

onto the tracks near her home, she sued the company for damages. The CPR refused to accept responsibility on grounds that a "No Trespassing" sign was prominently displayed near the scene. "Right," said Mother Fulham in her rebuttal. "And I suppose you thought my cow could read?"

4. **Chief Buffalo Child Long Lance.** An impostor masquerading as a Blackfoot Chief (real name, Sylvester Long) hired by the Calgary Herald to write about Native life on the reserves around Calgary. When he moved to the city hall beat, he decided to liven things up by donning a mask and rolling a fuse-lit "bomb" into council chambers. His richly detailed story made the front page the next day. Two days later, he was fingered as the culprit in the bomb hoax and fired. He became the first and only reporter in Herald history to have his dismissal recorded on the front page.

5. **Pearl Miller.** The most notorious brothel keeper in Calgary history. On the eve of the Normandy invasion in 1944, a group of American soldiers camped next to a regiment of Canadian soldiers from Calgary. The Americans tacked up a sign on the wall of their sergeants' mess that read, "Remember Pearl Harbor." The Calgarians responded by putting up their own sign: "To hell with Pearl Harbour, remember Pearl Miller."

1932: The Co-operative Commonwealth Federation (CCF) is founded in Calgary.

1932: Gasoline-fueled buses are introduced to serve areas without streetcar service.

1933: The Glenmore dam, reservoir and treatment plant opens.

1935: Calgary plays host to the First Social Credit convention, the political movement lead by the flamboyant William "Bible Bill" Aberhart.

1939: Calgary Municipal Airport opens.

1945: The Calgary Stampeders play their first game at Mewata Stadium. The team blanks the Regina Roughriders 12-0.

1947: W.O. Mitchell publishes his beloved book *Who Has Seen the Wind*.

1948: The Calgary Stampeders win the Grey Cup.

1948: 170 war brides from Britain arrive in Calgary.

1950: The Calgary Transit System retires its last streetcar.

1954: Alberta's first television station, CHCT-TV, broadcasts in Calgary.

1956: Calgary gets its first parking structure, the Hudson's Bay Parkade.

1960: The University of Alberta opens a new campus in Calgary.

1964: Calgary annexes the three satellite towns of Forest Lawn, Montgomery and Bowness.

1966: The University of Alberta in Calgary becomes the fully autonomous University of Calgary.

1967: An urban renewal program with a price tag of $21 million is announced. Over the next decade numerous historic buildings are torn down, making way for major projects such as the school board complexes, Glenbow Museum and Calgary Convention Centre as well as bank and oil company towers.

1968: In June, the 182 metre 10,884 tonne Husky Tower is opened in Calgary. It instantly becomes the most recognizable landmark in the city.

Sandstone City

Calgary has endured some ferocious fires. A January 1885 house fire inspired town officials to establish a bucket brigade and buy a fire engine. Tragically, this engine was sitting in a warehouse, held captive because of unpaid duty, and could not help extinguish the flames that ripped through the town on November 7, 1886. The inferno claimed most of the downtown business section and caused $100,200 in damages. In the aftermath, town council passed an ordinance stipulating that all downtown buildings be constructed of the abundant Paskapoo sandstone.

Fifteen quarries in the Calgary area supplied a sandstone construction boom as schools, churches and even City Hall were made of the material. These stone edifices came to symbolize Calgary, and gave the western city an air of permanence that was lacking in other frontier towns. The town's unique appearance earned it the favourable nickname "Sandstone City." The outbreak of World War I undermined these building trends, however, as men who staffed sandstone quarries left to serve in the armed forces.

1973: Thanks to the Arab Oil Embargo, Calgary's economy booms.

1975: The federal government launches the National Energy Policy designed to create a stronger Canadian presence in the oil industry. The policy casts a chill over the oil patch and creates an almost irreversible antipathy toward the Liberal Party.

1975: On May 8th, the last trolley buses run.

1975: Calgary hosts the Grey Cup for the first time.

1976: The nine million dollar Glenbow Centre, housing the Glenbow Museum, Art Gallery, Library and Archives, opens in Calgary.

1980: On January 12th, Calgarian skier Ken Read wins a World Cup downhill race on the famous course at Kitzbuhel, Austria.

1980: Ralph Klein is elected mayor of Calgary.

1982: Laurie Skreslet becomes the first Calgarian to climb Mount Everest.

1988: On February 13th, Canadian Governor General Jeanne Sauvé opens the 15th Winter Olympics in Calgary. The games, which bring together 1,800 athletes from 57 nations, are dubbed one of the most successful to date.

1989: The Calgary Flames defeat the Montreal Canadiens to win the Stanley Cup.

1991: City water is fluoridated for the first time.

1992: It's a winning year as the Calgary Stampeders win the Grey Cup and Calgary-raised Mark Tewksbury wins gold in the 100m backstroke at the Barcelona Summer Olympics.

2000: The World Petroleum Congress is held in Calgary.

2002: On Valentines Day, Calgarian Catriona Le May Doan wins gold in the women's 500m speed skating at the Salt Lake City Olympic Games.

2002: In July, G8 leaders meet in Calgary, filling the city with protestors, reporters and security officials.

2004: The Calgary Flames go to the seventh game of the Stanley Cup finals, losing 2-1 to the Tampa Bay Lightning. During the series, celebrating fans take over 17th Avenue SW which becomes known as 'the Red Mile.'

2005: The Bow and Elbow rivers flood, leading to widespread evacuations and causing $400 million in damages. It is the most expensive natural disaster in Alberta's history.

2007: The Calgary economy continues to lead the country. Average home prices reach unprecedented records.

Calgary Essentials

Location: In the foothills of Alberta's Rocky Mountains, at the junction of the Bow and Elbow Rivers.

Origin of Name: Calgary was named by Lieutenant-Colonel James Farquharson MacLeod of the North West Mounted Police in 1876. He took the name from the estate of the same name on the Isle of Mull, the ancestral home of his Scottish cousins, the MacKenzies.

Official Name: Heart of the New West (according to the Calgary Economic Development Corporation).

City Nicknames: Cow Town, Stampede City, C-Dot.

Official Flower: In 1991, the city adopted the Red Pasque Flower (*Anemone pulsatilla "Rubra"*) as its floral emblem. This flower is a fitting symbol for Calgary as it closely resembles the Prairie Crocus which grows in the Calgary area. Unlike the Prairie Crocus, the Red Pasque Flower has been hybridized and can be grown by gardeners.

They Said It

Official Flag: Calgary's official flag was designed by Gwin Clarke and Yvonne Fritz and was adopted in 1983 as a result of a contest. The design contains a cowboy hat and the letter "C" on a red background. The stetson has a hand-like shape and is a symbol of hospitality.

Calgary's Crest: Calgary's crest, adopted in 1902, was again the result of a contest. The upper third of the crest shows the setting sun above a mural crown — a symbol of loyalty — and the Rocky Mountains. The lower two-thirds bear the red cross of St. George and the Canadian maple leaf inset by a bull buffalo, all supported by a horse and steer. Below the shield are the Canadian maple leaf, the leek of Wales, the shamrock of Ireland, the rose of England and the thistle of Scotland.

Calgary's Motto: Onward

Dates of Incorporation: As a town: 1884; as a city: 1894.

Time Zone: Mountain Standard Time

Area Code: 403

Postal Codes: T1Y to T3R

System of Measurement: Metric

Voting Age: 18

Drinking Age: 18

Statutory Holidays: The province of Alberta has nine official statutory holidays: Christmas Day, New Year's Day, Remembrance Day, Victoria Day, Labour Day, Canada Day, Thanksgiving Day and Alberta Family Day (the third Monday in February). As well, many Calgary businesses allow workers to take off the morning of the Calgary Stampede parade, held the first Friday in July after Canada Day.

Take 5 GERRY MEEK AND STAFF'S TOP FIVE ESSENTIAL READS

Gerry Meek is the Director of Calgary Public Library. The Calgary Public Library system has 17 locations and is Canada's 2nd largest system. When all types of users are combined, Calgarians used the Library more than 32 million times in 2006. The Central Library, the heart and hub of the system, is located in downtown Calgary adjacent to City Hall and Olympic Plaza. Gerry, along with many other staff members, chose what they believe are the top five books that provide intriguing insight to the city and its' people.

1. *Calgary: Spirit of the West* by Hugh Dempsey. Published by the Glenbow and Fifth House Ltd, 1994.
2. *Historic Walks of Calgary* by Harry Sanders. Published by Red Deer Press, 2005.
3. *Calgary: Heart of the New West*, introduction by Darrel Janz. Published by Towery Publications, 2001.
4. *Udderly Art: Colourful Cows for Calgary* by Tom Keyser. Published by Johnson Gorman, 2000.
5. *Fields of Fire: An Illustrated History of Canadian Petroleum* by David Finch and Gordon Jaremko. Published by Detselig Enterprises Ltd, 1995.

SISTER CITIES

The city of Calgary has no fewer than six 'sister cities' around the world. The first city into which it entered such a relationship was Quebec City in 1956, followed in 1973 by Jaipur, India. In 1985, Daqing, China came into the family, as did Naucalpan, Mexico in 1994. Daejeon, South Korea signed on in 1996 and the following year saw Pheonix, Arizona enter the fold.

AREA

Calgary: 722 km^2
Toronto: 641 km^2
New York: 831 km^2

Elevation: 1,128 m

Number of Parks: 29

PATHWAYS

For a city built on the consumption of fossil fuels, it might come as a surprise to discover that Calgary is home to the largest urban pathway system in North America. The network encompasses more than 600 km of dedicated recreational pathways and over 250 km of shared on-street bikeways.

LANGUAGES WE SPEAK

- Percentage whose mother tongue is English: 78
- Chinese (Mandarin, Cantonese, etc.): 4.4
- Italian: 1.6
- German: 1.6

Did you know...

that there are more than 25,000 more single men in Calgary than there are single women?

They Said It

> "It's a good music town. I knew some players out here. Nice people. (I also like) how many Maritimers there are out here. There's a pile of them even from my own hometown. I love the mountains - that's the other thing I really love about out here."
>
> **– Dylan MacDonald on what he likes most about his adopted Calgary.**

- French: 1.6
- Punjabi: 1.4
- Other languages include — Polish, Spanish, Portuguese, Ukrainian, Arabic, Dutch, Tagalog, Greek, Vietnamese, Cree, Inuktitut
- Percentage of Calgarians who are bilingual: 1.3

Source: Statistics Canada

LIFE EXPECTANCY AT BIRTH

	Alberta	Canada
Male	77.5	77.4
Female	82.2	82.4
Total	79.9	79.9

Source: Alberta Government.

POPULATION

Population of the City of Calgary: 988,193
Population of the Municipality: 1,079,310

Source: Statistics Canada

Did you know...

that Calgary has more than 180 distinct neighbourhoods within its boundaries?

POPULATION IN PERSPECTIVE

Calgary is the fifth largest municipality in Canada — after Toronto, Montreal, Vancouver and Ottawa. Its population of one million makes it about a fifth the size of Toronto (5.3 million).

Calgary has about as many people as the small nations of Trinidad & Tobago (1,088,600) and East Timor (1,040,900), and has about a quarter of the population of Ireland (four million).

Take 5 WILL FERGUSON'S TOP FIVE THINGS
YOU MAY NOT KNOW ABOUT CALGARY

Will Ferguson was born and raised in Alberta. An author, humorist and historian, he has traveled the world, recounting in ten books and countless newspaper and magazine columns his adventures abroad and offering his perspectives on his home country.

Ferguson's first book, a tale of reverse-culture shock titled *Why I Hate Canadians*, sold more than 50,000 copies. The follow-up, *How to Be Canadian*, has sold more than 200,000 copies and was awarded the CBA Libris Award for Non-Fiction Book of the Year. His *Canadian History for Dummies* won the Canadian Authors Association Award for History. His book *Happiness and How to Be a Canadian* were short-listed for the Stephen Leacock Medal for Humour, the first time an author had been nominated twice in one year. *Happiness* took home the prize as did his *Beauty Tips from Moose Jaw* in 2005. Ferguson was also awarded the Pierre Berton Award by Canada's National History Society. He lives in Calgary with his wife Terumi and their two sons.

1. Calgary is one of the most educated cities in Canada, nudged out only by Ottawa in the number of postgraduate degrees. Instead of bestowing visitors with a white hat, perhaps we should be giving them honorary degrees instead. That would certainly reflect Calgary's demographics more accurately. There's a good deal more MBAs in this city than cowboys.

2. Calgary is a heartland for volunteerism. You may have heard this claim before. Well, it's true. The Canadian Centre for Philanthropy

CALGARY JOINS THE MILLION CLUB

On July 24, 2006, Calgary welcomed its millionth bouncing baby citizen. Dashiell Waite, weighing in at nine pounds, ten ounces, was welcomed into the world by a host of business and community leaders, including Mayor Dave Bronconnier who celebrated the occasion by white hatting the wee tyke. Instead of the usual wide brimmed Stetson bestowed on visiting dignitaries and notables, little Dashiell was given a specially knitted white cap with "Calgary One Million" embroidered across the front.

has reported that Calgarians donate 50 percent more to charities than the national average, and far ahead of Toronto. This is a "booster city" in the best sense, and even at one million people, Calgary still has that civic spirit.

3. Calgary has one of the highest Green Party votes in Canada, second only to Victoria. In fact, three out of Calgary's eight ridings gave the Green Party more than 10 per cent support – a significant milestone for the environmental movement. Maybe Elizabeth May should have run in Calgary Centre instead?

4.Despite its public image, Calgary is a green city. Montreal's Maisonneuve Magazine has stated that "Calgary's commitment to green power is the largest in North America," with commitments in place for the city to run on 75 percent green sources (such as wind power), with greenhouse gas emissions to be cut by 50 percent below its 1990 levels within five years. No other city in Canada – or the continent – can match this.

5. Calgary has a break-out theatre scene. Following the trail blazed by Edmonton, Calgary has embraced new and innovative theatre. This is a young city with an optimistic air. It's a city open to new ideas, something reflected in what is now one of the strongest arts and new theatre scenes in Canada. When Douglas Coupland launched his one-man play *September 10, A Play* he chose Calgary for its debut.

YOU KNOW YOU'RE FROM

- Your belt buckle cost more than your watch.
- You've rubbed shoulders with Ralph Klein at the Louis.
- Drinking your weight in beer during the Stampede is considered a virtue.
- You not only own a Stetson, you know how to wear it.
- You know the difference between Smithbilt and Peterbilt.
- You know the difference between MacKenzie Towne and Chapparal.
- You spend more money on Stampede entertainment than Christmas.
- You know someone who has been a Young Canadian.
- Two-stepping is something you're good at, and proud of.
- You know what bitumen means.
- You own at least one Flames jersey.
- You've considered naming your firstborn Iggy or Kipper.
- You've volunteered with at least one organization in the last year.
- You know the Plus 15's like the back of your hand.
- You ride your bike/Vespa/motorcycle after the first snowfall.
- You know the difference between the Ship and the Drum.
- You've been to the Stampede parade at least once without any sleep.
- You can recite the names of the current Stampede Queen and Princesses.
- You know that Bronco is the mayor's nickname.
- You think the Flames were robbed in the 2004 Stanley Cup final game.
- Your idea of an awesome night on the town includes a shisha bar, burlesque dancing and honkytonks.
- You've written at least one letter to the editor of the *Calgary Herald*.
- A mini-Hummer makes sense.
- You're hung over for most of July.
- Jeans and a button down shirt are "business casual."
- You've puked in a bathroom at Cowboy's that wasn't designated for your gender.
- Going to the Deep South means driving to Shawnessy.
- Someone in your family is an engineer or a geologist.

CALGARY WHEN...

- A $350,000 condo is a steal.
- You've stumbled the Red Mile.
- Chanteuse Jann Arden has served you meatloaf and Jell-O.
- You still call it the Husky Tower.
- Oil and gas guru Gwen Morgan has flipped you pancakes.
- Golf is a legitimate business expense.
- You wear snow boots one week and sandals the next.
- You've made out while watching the fireworks from Scotsman's Hill.
- Skinny-dipping in the Bow is a rite of passage.
- You religiously attend Cowboy church during Stampede, even though you're Jewish.
- You think urban sprawl means stretching out in a buddy's down-town loft.
- There's a photo of you and Ralph having a beer at the Cecil.
- Crescent Road conjures images of first kisses and midnight tobog-gan runs.
- Patio time means cruising 17th Ave for a good spot to sit.
- You wear a business suit to a fashion gala.
- Dark blue is NOT the only acceptable colour for a business suit.
- Climate change is either the next best thing, or a Liberal conspira-cy to shackle the West.
- Eating at home means ordering in.
- Cappuccinos at Lina's Italian Market is a Saturday ritual.
- Fear of Deerfoot is a seasonal driving disorder starting with the first snowfall.
- You accept city council making more than any other council in Canada, and voting themselves a 10 percent raise.
- You are equally as comfortable at Ceasar's Steakhouse as at Tekko Sushi.
- You buy ground bison from the Co-op to make burgers.
- Out east means anything past Winnipeg.
- Lunch at the Petroleum Club every Tuesday is non-negotiable.
- You know your way around Houston.
- Visiting friends and family make it out to the mountains more often than you do.

Did you know...

that the Calgary Zoo is the second largest in Canada? Kamala, the zoo's elephant matriarch, has gained a reputation as a talented painter and her work is often auctioned off, raising money for various charities in the city.

POPULATION DENSITY
- Calgary: 1,279 people/km^2
- Edmonton: 1,047 people/km^2
- Toronto: 3,939/km^2
- New York City: 10,194 people/km^2
- Tokyo: 13,416 people/km^2

UP AND UP
Over the past five years, the population of Calgary has increased by 12.4 percent, outpacing Canada's growth rate of 5.4 percent and Alberta's of 10.6 percent.

Median Age
34.9 years

BOYS AND GIRLS (2006)

	Men	Women
Total	497,449	494,310
0-19	123,166	119,172
20-34	120,197	120,309
35-64	212, 224	202,832
64+	41,862	51,997

Source: City of Calgary.

Did you know...

that 20.9 percent of Calgarians are foreign born?

CRADLE TO GRAVE
- Number of Calgarians born in 2005: 12,910
- Number of deaths: 4,680
- Number of marriages: 4,536

Source: Alberta Government.

MARITAL STATUS
(Population aged 15 and over)
- Percentage who are married: 51
- Percentage who are single: 34
- Percentage divorced: 8
- Percentage separated: 3
- Widowed: 4

MEAN AGE AT FIRST MARRIAGE IN ALBERTA
Men: 33.1 (Canada: 34.6)
Women 30.7 (Canada, 32.1)

Source: Statistics Canada.

CATS AND DOGS (2006)
- Number of dogs in Calgary: 92,563
- Number of cats: 90,137

Source: City of Calgary

Did you know...

that in 2006, Calgary saw its total population increase by 35,681. Of these, 9,887 came from natural increase, the remaining 25,794 from in-migration.

They Said It

RELIGION

Calgary is often said to be in the "Bible Beltbuckle." This play on words is said to reflect the jeans-wearing cowboys and the high number of Christian conservatives who call Calgary and Southern Alberta home.

RELIGIOUS AFFILIATION

- Percentage who are Protestant: 35.2
- Percentage who are Catholic: 26.3
- Percentage with no religious affiliation: 25.2
- Christian (not affiliated): 4.3
- Muslim: 2.7
- Christian Orthodox: 1.2
- Buddhist: 1.7
- Sikh: 1.4
- Hindu: .07
- Jewish: .06
- Eastern religions: .01
- Other religions: .02

Source: Statistics Canada.

Did you know...

that Calgary grows at a rate of 98 new arrivals a day (35,770 a year)?

HEALTH CARE

Calgary has three major hospitals: the Foothills Medical Centre, the Rockyview General Hospital and the Peter Lougheed Centre, all overseen by the Calgary Health Region. A medical evacuation helicopter (Stars Air Ambulance) operates under the auspices of the Shock Trauma Rescue Safety.

Calgary also has the Tom Baker Cancer Centre (located in the Foothills Medical Centre), the Alberta Children's Hospital and the Grace Women's Health Centre providing a variety of care, in addition to hundreds of smaller medical and dental clinics. The University of Calgary Medical Centre also operates in partnership with the Calgary Health Region.

EMERGENCY MEDICAL SERVICES

The City of Calgary Emergency Medical Services (EMS) experiences over 96,000 emergency responses a year, and operates 44 advanced life support (ALS) response vehicles during peak times.

Source: City of Calgary Emergency Medical Services.

• Number of Doctors in Calgary: 2,603

Source: College of Physicians and Surgeons of Alberta.

SCHOOLS

• Number of schools under the Calgary Catholic School District: 98
• Estimated staff: 4,000
• Estimated number of students: 44,000
• Number of schools under the Calgary Board of Education: 219

Did you know...

that 80 percent of Calgarians are proud of their downtown and 77 percent think that Calgary has a good quality of life?

- Estimated number of teaching staff: 5,500
- Estimated number of support and CUPE staff: 3,000
- Estimated number of students: 98,380

Source: Calgary Board of Education.

SECONDARY EDUCATION

Calgary is home to several universities and colleges.

- The University of Calgary, home to 28,807 students, is Calgary's largest degree-granting facility.
- Mount Royal College is the city's second largest institution with an enrollment of 13,000.
- Bow Valley College provides training in business, technology and the liberal arts for about 10,000 students.
- The Southern Alberta Institute of Technology (SAIT) provides polytechnic education.
- The Alberta College of Art and Design (ACAD) offers training in the arts.
- University of Lethbridge has a satellite campus in Calgary.
- There also several private liberal arts institutions including Alliance University College, Nazarene University College and St. Mary's University College.
- Calgary is home to DeVry Career College's only Canadian campus.
- Also in Calgary: The Alberta Bible College and Rocky Mountain College.

Source: UnivSource.

PROFESSIONAL SPORTS TEAMS AND THEIR NOTABLE WINS

- Flames, National Hockey League: 1 Stanley Cup Championship
- Stampeders, Canadian Football League: 5 Championships
- Roughnecks, National Lacrosse League: 1 Championship
- Vipers, Northern League (baseball): 0 Championships

Major Daily Newspapers: *Calgary Herald* and the *Calgary Sun*

Weblinks

The City of Calgary

www.calgary.ca

Everything you want to know about Calgary, from job opportunities to traffic updates to the comprehensive A to Z Directory.

Calgary Economic Development

www.calgaryeconomicdevelopment.com

Find out about the region's competitive advantages, pro business climate and superior lifestyle.

The Calgary Herald

www.canada.com/calgaryherald

A daily newspaper with free archives. The site is updated each day.

Slang:

Calgary's cowboy culture, oil patch connections and rich assortment of new citizens from around the world have created a distinct and colourful local dialect. From disparaging references to Edmonton, to nicknames for politicians, there's no shortage of peppery language to get the point across.

Arrow, the: Refers to the Red Arrow Bus Line that is the usual mode of transportation for Jug Hounds going to the Patch.

Barneys: When locals say they're going to pick up some Barneys, they are referring to good ol' KFC.

Bible Beltbuckle: A common term referring to the idea that a disproportionate number of Christian conservatives call Calgary and Southern Alberta home.

Bronco: Nickname for Calgary's 35th Mayor, Dave Bronconnier.

Buckle Bunny: A less than flattering term for rodeo and bull busting groupies.

Buddy: A friend. Also used as a general pronoun, as in "Hey buddy, down in front!"

Burnout: Refers either to the act of spinning a vehicle's tires on the spot, or someone who has become mentally unfit through drug or alcohol consumption.

Calgary Red Eye: Not an eye malady, this drink made of beer and clamato juice is an acquired taste.

C-Dot: A term for Calgary that was modeled after T-Dot, a name referencing Toronto.

C-Train: Calgary's Light Rail Transit System. When asking locals directions they won't think twice before saying, "Just hop a C-Train to Anderson and the mall is right across the street."

Cow Town: Often used by tourists, visitors and people from Edmonton.

Cow Pie: A fresh pile of cow dung.

Chin-ache: refers to the headaches often brought on by the barometric pressure changes in Chinooks.

Deadmonton: A derogatory name for that other Albertan city. You know, the one with the mall.

Derrick: Perhaps also the name of your third cousin, in the oil biz this is the tall tower on a drilling rig.

Doghouse: In Calgary this does not just mean the punishment you deserve because you forgot your wife's birthday; it is also the small building on a drill site where oil rig workers can sit for dinner or just a break.

Flat: Elsewhere known as a "two-four" or a "case," in Calgary this is a package of 24 cans of beer. Bottles sold in packs of 24 do not earn the name as the word comes from the low, flat surface formed by a package of 24 beer cans.

Foothills: Although not technically a slang term, the foothills refer to the rolling hills that separate the prairie from the mountains.

Take 5 — WRITER AND POET VIVAN HANSEN'S FIVE CALGARY INSPIRED PHRASES

Vivian Hansen was born in 1957 to Danish immigrants. As a writer and poet, she has been published widely in Canadian journals, and has tackled such issues as women's rights, immigration, work and the western landscape. Her chapbook of poetry *Never Call It Bird: the Melodies of Aids* came out in 1998. Her first full-length book of poetry *Leylines of My Flesh* was published by Touchwood Press in 2002, and two years later she published *Angel Alley*, a chapbook about the victims of Jack the Ripper. Awards she has won include the Arrol Award for Nonfiction and the Self-Connection Book Award.

1. "These calloused sandstone outcroppings are the teeth of Nose Hill."

2. "On Nose Hill, the wind holds Power and Medicine."

3. "Tadpole choirs in pools."

4. "The fine fur of a weasel, dreamed into a poplar stump."

5. "Shape-shifting deer in dun poplars."

Howdy: Old-school cowboy(girl) greeting, especially prominent during the Calgary Stampede.

Get 'Er Done: A self-explanatory example of Calgary's 'can do' attitude.

Givin 'Er: Driving really fast or drinking heavily.

Gong Show: Popularized by Ralph Klein, it refers to a social situation that is out of control.

The Jube: The Jubilee Auditorium. The sister building in Edmonton goes by the same name. Together, they are the Jubes.

Jug Hound: Yet another oil patch term, referring to the workers (hounds) who distribute geophones across broad swaths of land to help determine the location of potential oil finds.

Kleinisms: A term referring to the many colourful statements for which former Calgary mayor and former Albertan Premier, Ralph Klein, is (in)famously known.

MFWIC: A rather colourful acronym for the oil patch describing the person in charge – usually when something goes wrong (mother f#$%er who's in charge.)

Mogas: Oil industry slang for motor gasoline.

Navaho Mug: International recording artist Ian Tyson owns a coffee shop just south of the city – if you're ordering a cup of joe down in those parts, order a Navaho Mug.

No Doubt: An affirmative response to a statement that doesn't require a response.

Oilfield Trash: A pejorative name for the large number of oil workers who flock to oil fields "from away."

Oil Patch: Sweeping term for all forms of business related to Calgary's booming oil and gas industry.

Plus 15: Calgary's intricate web of pathways connecting the downtown. They originally started at 15 ft above street level.

Prairie Oysters: Yum yum. The testicles of a bull, sliced off during the steering process. They are still served in select Calgary restaurants.

Rat Patrol: Alberta is the world's largest rat-free landmass, and the Rat Patrol is here to make sure it stays that way.

Ralph Bucks: Government surplus cheques of $400 distributed to taxpayers beginning in 2005.

Red Mile: Seventeenth Avenue earned its nickname after swarms of fans in red jerseys took over the street during the Stanley Cup playoff run of 2004.

Rig and Dig: The equipment used by an oil drilling operation.

Rocksniffer: The geologists on an oil drill site.

Rough Neck: An oil rig worker, often seen as rough around the edges. It is also the name of Calgary's Lacrosse Team.

Runners: To the rest of the world, they're referred to as sneakers or tennis shoes. Here they're referred to as runners.

Skid: Someone with a rough appearance.

Skol Ring: For years, cowboys have had a reputation for partaking in the habit of chewing tobacco or snuff. It comes in a round plastic case which tends to leave a circular impression in ones Wranglers.

Smokie: You may have had hotdogs, franks, footlongs, handwarmers, weiners or a variety of other names for one of the world's most favourite foods. In Cow Town, it's Smokies that'll draw a crowd around a BBQ.

Spolumbos: Well, where can I get a Smokie, you ask. Spolumbos Fine Meats has become such a household brand in Calgary that if someone tells you to pick up some Spolumbos, you know you're invited to a party in their backyard.

Stubble Jumper: A common term used to describe a transplant hailing from the flat province of Saskatchewan. It conjures images of a lad running through a freshly harvested wheat field.

Supercan: A large, pint-size can of beer.

Tallboy, tallie: A supercan.

Toolpush: The person in charge of an oil rig.

Trad: Traditional Ale, a beer brewed by Big Rock Brewery in Calgary.

Trail: I don't know if it has anything to do with the pioneer attitude of the west but you won't find many throughfares and parkways here. The major routes have such colourful names as Deerfoot Trail, Crowfoot Trail, Stoney Trail and so on.

Turn Down the Suck: From the 2003 film *"Fubar"*, filmed in Calgary, meaning something is of poor quality.

Wood, the: Calgarians go to the Wood (Ironwood Stage & Grill) when they're craving some good live music.

Worm: The lowest member of the drilling crew. Generally this person works the "break-out" or lead tongs on the left side of the drilling floor.

Yeehaw: An expression of cow person exuberance used most often during the Stampede.

Urban Geography

Five hundred and forty four million years ago, the area where Calgary stands today was part of the Pacific Ocean. As sedimentary rocks pushed up to form the Rocky Mountains, it formed an inland sea which over eons became filled with sediment.

Over the last two million years there have been a number of glacial periods when most of Canada became covered with thick glacial ice. The most recent of these periods occurred about twenty thousand years ago. A huge ice sheet from central and northern Canada (Laurentide Ice Sheet) met with Cordilleran glaciers flowing eastward out of valleys in the Rocky Mountains. They met along a line that passes through present day Calgary.

The heart of the present day city lies where the Bow and Elbow rivers meet after flowing down from the Rocky Mountains and winding through the Foothills. The landscape is the product of ancient mountain building, succeeding ice ages, and river erosion.

LATITUDE AND LONGITUDE

Calgary is located at 51°6'N latitude and 114°1'W longitude. Those numbers put the city along the same horizontal lines as Amsterdam, Berlin and Warsaw, and along the same vertical lines as Las Vegas and Phoenix.

TWO RIVERS RUN THROUGH IT

Calgary is built along the banks of two rivers – the Bow and the Elbow. The Bow originates at Bow Glacier and is more than 623 km long. The upper river is a white water torrent, but by the time it reaches Calgary it has quieted significantly.

The Elbow River is also a mountain river. It originates at Elbow Lake in the Elbow-Sheep Wildland Provincial Park. From its source it flows down the mountains, through the foothills and into the hamlet of Bragg Creek. The river enters Calgary at the Weaselhead Flats, an artificial inland delta, and flows into the Glenmore Reservoir, one of Calgary's two main sources of drinking water. From there, it rolls northward through residential communities towards the city centre, passes the Stampede grounds and joins the Bow River.

These rivers are extremely important to the social and environmental fabric of the city. They provide valuable recreation areas and wildlife habitat, and are also the source of drinking water. In 1991, the River Valley's Committee (RVC) was formed to preserve these irreplaceable waterways.

FOUR SQUARE

Calgary's 722 km^2 are divided into four quadrants — Northwest, Northeast, Southwest and Southeast. In the Northwest portion of the city lies a mixture of older, established areas as well as newer, upscale developments. It's here that you'll find pricey housing, the University of Calgary and a gateway to the mountains.

Northeast Calgary also boasts a housing district, though more modest. Compared to the rest of the city, housing here costs less and the neighbourhoods are peppered with schools, playgrounds and parks.

Did you know...

that in 1993 the average price of a residential home in Calgary was $130,791?

Take 5   FIVE THINGS YOU CAN DO FOR FREE IN CALGARY

1. **The Pathways:** With approximately 635 km of pathways and 260 km of on-street bikeways within its boundaries, the city boasts the most extensive urban pathway and bikeway network in North America. Snow is cleared off 110 km of the pathway system during the winter months to ensure all-season access. Traveling the entire pathway system would require you to cross 67 bridges.

2. **C-train:** Let's be clear, not the entire route is free, but for the frugal traveler a trip downtown need not get your dogs barking. You can hop on and off the downtown portion (along 7th Ave.) as much as you like. Known as the "Poor Man's Tour," it's a great way to pack in the sites and shops of Calgary's core.

3. **Bow River Float:** Not for everyone, but a refreshing trip down the Bow is a great way to beat the summer heat in Cow Town. One should take heed though; a well marked weir by The Calgary Zoo is to be avoided. So pick your stopping point, have a ride waiting, and enjoy the wonderful sites and tranquility of Southern Alberta's main waterway.

4. **Eau Clair Market:** A great place to spend the day. Prince's Island Park in Eau Claire has lots of shaded picnic area with a great playground for the kids. Bring along a frisbee or football. The Island is home to Calgary's biggest musical event of the year - the Calgary Folk Festival.

5. **Devonian Gardens:** If the weather isn't co-operating with your plans, this little gem, located in TD Square is a great reprieve from the elements. Boasting a large variety of plant life, some of the largest and most colorful varieties of carp, plus collections of renowned artists from the region, Devonian Gardens feels like a walk in a tropical forest.

Did you know...

that the brown trout that thrive in the Bow River and attract fishers from around the world, found their home by accident? In 1925, a truck full of young trout broke down and the cargo found its way into the river. The rest, as they say, is history.

The Southeast district contains the historical core of the city, with original settlements dating back to the days of Fort Calgary. The area is known for its beautifully restored heritage properties and its award winning lake districts.

Finally, the Southwest area — which includes the downtown — is where all the action is. Prestigious areas such as Mount Royal and Elbow Park boast mansion quality architecture and breathtaking views of the mountains and the rest of the city.

PLANES, TRAINS AND...
- 445 bridges of the vehicle, pedestrian, rail and tunnel persuasion
- 79,000 streetlights
- 843 traffic signal lights
- 221 pedestrian corridor lights
- 125,292 traffic signs
- 4,671 km of curbs and gutters
- 4,793 km of sidewalks

Did you know...

that historical Stephen Avenue Walk, or Eighth Ave. S.W., was named after the Canadian Pacific Railway's first president, Lord George Mount Stephen and was officially declared a Canadian Historic site in 2002? Stretching from First Street S.E. to Fourth Street S.W. the street attracts 60,000 people during the lunch hour in the summer. With buskers, performance art and street vendors, it is a lively part of the city's urban fabric.

- 4,203 km of paved roads
- 84 km of oiled roads
- 7 km of concrete roads
- 366 km of paved lanes
- 1,081 km of graveled lanes

Source: City of Calgary.

The Fairmont Palliser Hotel

"These springs are worth a million dollars," were the words of Canadian Pacific Railway builder William Cornelius Van Horne upon seeing the Cave and Basin Hot Springs in Banff National Park. He was more than right of course. Visitors to Banff now drop almost a billion dollars annually.

If visitors from the South and East were going to make their way to Banff, chances were they would stop off in Calgary. And if you were going to wow them in Banff, you better wow them in Calgary too.

Enter the Fairmont Palliser Hotel, the grand dame of the city's hotels. Despite major renovations, you can still sense the turn of century grandeur. Public areas are fitted with oak paneling, candelabras, marble columns and floors, handmade rugs and public art. The 350 guest rooms feature mahogany doors, brass beds and windows. In a city largely devoid of glitz and glamour, the Palliser was a prescient sigh of wealth to come.

The Crystal Ballroom was the scene of many elegant dances over the years, but with the strict liquor laws of the early part of the 20th century galas were officially dry events. This prompted daring guests to smuggle in flasks of whiskey and mix their drinks under the cover of long white table linens.

Over the years the Palliser has been home to many important events. When Queen Elizabeth II visited Calgary in 2005, the Palliser became her home away from home, and Academy Award-winning director Ang Lee held his press conference in the lobby to promote his film, *Brokeback Mountain*.

Take 5 BEV SANDALACK'S TOP FIVE
RETAIL AND RESIDENTIAL STREETS IN CALGARY

Bev Sandalack is the founding coordinator of the Urban Design Program at the University of Calgary and the director of the Urban Lab at the faculty of Environmental Design. She has an award-winning research-based practice, and is co-author of *The Calgary Project: Urban form/Urban life*, and co-author of a column in the Calgary Herald on urban design and development.

Best Retail

1. **17th Avenue SW between 2nd Street and 10th Street** shows why Calgary's premiere urban space is a street and not a square — mixed use, high density, and relatively unscathed by the ravages of setbacks and urban renewal.

2. **4th Street SW between 21st Avenue and the Elbow River.** The same formula of mixed use, zero setback and surrounding residential density keeps this street vibrant, but sharply drops off north of 21st Avenue where the pattern changes.

3. **Kensington Avenue between 10th Street and 11A Street, and 10th Street between the Bow River and 3rd Avenue.** They are an inseparable couple — a small right-angled strip of pedestrian heaven, easy to get to (with the LRT stop right there it is the original transit oriented development), and surrounded by higher density residential.

4. **9th Avenue SE from 11th Street to 13th Street**. One of Calgary's original main streets, now a Saturday browsing par-

adise but still managing to keep with architect/politician Jack Long's KISS exhortation: Keep Inglewood Slightly Sleazy.

5. Stephen Avenue between 1st Street SE and 5th Street SW
Calgary's historic commercial street, architectural assortment, restaurant mecca and weekday people place, and one of the first experiments in shared pedestrian/vehicle space.

Best Residential

1. **Garden Crescent:** One-of-a-kind oasis near the Elbow River and 4th Street, showing that narrow streets do work.

2. **Bison Path:** Topographical, historical and eclectic, well worth the climb.

3. **Maggie Street:** House forms, setbacks and street character that still retain some of Ramsay's working-class background.

4. **13th Avenue between 1st Street SW and 17th Street SW:**
Perhaps the longest stretch in Calgary where you can walk on a continuous sidewalk under a canopy of trees, with a full range of housing types, a half-dozen parks and intersect several retail streets.

5. **Rideau Road / Roxboro Road:** Past some of the choicest spots along the Elbow River, and hooking up with the river path at either end.

They Said It

NUMBER ONE

- Rank of Calgary among the top cities worldwide in terms of health and cleanliness, according to a study conducted by Mercer Human Resource Consulting which measured the quality and availability of hospital and medical supplies and levels of air pollution and infectious diseases in 215 cities: 1
- Rank of Calgary in Mercer's broader "quality of life" survey: 24

URBAN OASIS

The city of Calgary maintains a veritable forest of trees, designed not only to beautify the city but also to clean the air. This did not come by chance, and it has taken a huge effort and massive expenditure to successfully grow the array of species now gracing Calgary's streets. Indeed, seven decades ago, just seven varieties of trees grew in Calgary. Today, the urban forest of Calgary boasts more than seventy different species. The city has a policy to promote further greening. Groups wishing to plant trees can participate in a 50-50 cost sharing program with Calgary Parks.

- Number of trees in the city's groomed parks and along streets: 350,000
- Per tree, the cost of this vegetation: $300-$30,000
- Total value of the city's greenery: $335,000,000

Source: City of Calgary.

Take 5 CALGARY'S FIVE
BEST KEPT SECRETS

1. **The Naval Museum of Alberta:** A naval museum in a land-locked province? Yes, and with the largest collection of documents and displays from the battles in the Atlantic and Pacific Oceans. The Naval Museum of Alberta is an informative and fun way for families to commemorate the achievements and sacrifices of the many men and women who gave their lives during a time of need.

2. **Heritage Park:** A rare glimpse into the past, Heritage Park offers children and adults alike a view of frontier life at the turn of the century. From a steam locomotive, to a blacksmith shop and a paddle boat on the reservoir, the park has something for everyone.

3. **Calgary Tower:** Although somewhat dwarfed these days, the Calgary Tower offers visitors an unparalleled view of the city from the prairies to the foothills to the mountains. With a revolving restaurant and clear floor one can experience the whole city while sitting down to a fine meal.

4. **Telus World of Science:** With over 263,000 visitors, how can it still be a secret? School trips from around the province make an annual pilgrimmage here. With a hands on approach to learning, you find parents having as much or more fun than the children. With its planetarium and indoor and outdoor activities, one can easily spend a whole day taking in the exhibits.

5. **Bowness Park:** A year-round paradise, Bowness Park will have you harkening back to a simpler rockwellian time. Whether skating on the lagoon in winter with a cup of hot chocolate or paddle boating and mini golfing, this park — with its fountains and tree lined fields along the Bow River — is a fun and relaxing way to spend a day.

Take 5 FIVE DOWNTOWN CALGARY

TOURIST ATTRACTIONS

1. **Fort Calgary Historic Park**
2. **Devonian Gardens**
3. **Stephen Avenue Walk Historic District**
4. **Chinatown**
5. **Eau Claire Festival Market District**

PARK IT!

More than ten percent of Calgary's land area is parkland and open spaces. The city boasts 40 parks — including 29 major ones — covering a total area of 7,500 hectares. Some of the bigger parks located in the downtown area include Olympic Plaza, Century Gardens and Bow River Promenade.

WALKING THE WALK

If you decided to walk or bike the pedestrian and bicycle pathways' entire length, you would cross 67 bridges, read more than 750 signs and keep your speed to a respectable 20 km/h. The city ensures that snow is cleared off 110 km of the system so that users have access during the winter months.

DOWNTOWN

Calgary's downtown is the city's financial centre. One of every five Calgarians work downtown and nearly 130,000 people live within five kilometers of the central business district. With about 35 million square feet of office space, downtown Calgary is home to 3,500 busi-

Did you know...

that the Calgary International Airport is Canada's fourth largest, receiving 9.2 million passengers each year?

nesses and 124 commercial office buildings.

Downtown boasts more than 1,000 retail stores, 11 indoor shopping centres, over 200 eateries, about 50 nightclubs and 10 cinemas, and hosts 25 major festivals each year. Downtown is also only 20 minutes from the airport and 40 minutes during rush hour from the city's edge.

Source: Downtown Calgary.

Towering?

On June 29, 1968, the Husky Tower was officially opened by then-Premier Ernest Manning. "Calgary will never be forgotten by visitors because of this distinctive tower," he said in his remarks. The Husky Tower enjoyed the distinction of being Canada's tallest building for just four months. Later that same year the Toronto Dominion building took away that title. In 1983, the completion of the Petro-Canada building unseated the tower's claim as Calgary's tallest building.

It doesn't matter to Calgarians. The tower remains the single most recognizable landmark in the city, and it foretells the economic promise of the city. The tower was a joint venture between Husky Oil and Marathon Realty and was built beginning in February 1967 to celebrate Canada's Centennial.

The project cost only $3.5 million. It was the first western Canadian building constructed to withstand earthquakes —the tower can sway 16.5 cm on windy days. In case of emergencies there are two 802-step staircases available — these staircases have also hosted endurance races and climbers training for Mount Everest.

In 1971, the name of the structure changed from Husky Tower to the Calgary Tower. The tower celebrates when Calgarians do. This was especially true in 1988, when a gas-fired caldron was affixed to the top of the observation deck so that the tower could mimic the Olympic torch that burned in the city for the winter games. Since the 1988 Olympics, the "torch" has been lit to celebrate New Years, special events and the Stanley Cup playoffs.

PLUS 15

A series of 57 connected bridges, roughly 15 feet above the street, connect the gleaming towers of downtown Calgary, keeping office workers, wanderers and shoppers warm in winter and cool in summer. The system, which was started in 1970 when a link was built between the Westin Hotel and Calgary Place, is 16 km long.

Plus 15 was created to provide a convenient way for office workers to travel the downtown without having to face bad weather or bad drivers at street level. Today the Plus 15 (and the higher Plus 30 and Plus 45) system in Calgary is the largest of its kind in the world.

In addition to eateries, the Plus 15 hosts top boutiques, medical centres, theatre groups, movies and bars. It has even served as the backdrop for the dark comedy *Waydowntown*, about a group of office workers who bet on who can stay within the Plus 15 the longest without venturing outside.

The arts community has embraced the walkways as a place to showcase a wide variety of work, and it's a pleasant diversion from the hustle and bustle of downtown life.

New buildings are required to provide Plus 15 access as part of their building permit, and if they can't, then they have to pay into a Plus 15 Fund which is used to create other connections.

Critics of the system focus on the negative effect that the Plus 15 has had on street-level businesses and development.

WASTING AWAY

The City of Calgary plans to reduce by 20 percent the waste it puts in landfills. Residential waste for the city has remained at the same levels since 1993, despite a 23 percent increase in population.

Did you know...

that 42 percent of downtown commuters use public transit?

Did you know...

that Nose Hill Park's name is rumored to have come from Aboriginals who thought the area looked like the shape of their chief's nose?

- Calgary's households produce 33 percent of the city's waste.
- Construction, renovation and demolition are responsible for 27 percent, the rest being generated by industrial, commercial and institutional.
- Calgarians throw out nearly 4,000 tonnes of waste each week.
- Of all the residential waste that ends up in Calgary's landfills:
  - 27 percent is collected for paper recycling
  - 24 percent is collected as yard waste
  - 20 percent is collected as food waste
  - 2, 3 and 9 percent is recyclable glass, metal and plastic waste
- A 2003 electronics recycling 'round-up' collected 220,000 kg of material, setting a North American record.

Source: City of Calgary.

THE TRANSIT SYSTEM
- Calgary's transit system boasts 300 regular buses, 404 low-floor buses, 94 community shuttle buses and 116 light rail vehicles.
- Number of people served: 956,078
- Number of routes: 160
- Number of route kilometers: 4,571
- Annual number of boarding passengers: 119.5 million
- Revenue earned in 2005: $82.0 million

Source: Calgary Transit.

Did you know...

that Calgary has 47 recycling depots?

WHERE TO PLAY

- Number of athletic parks in Calgary: 11
- Number of aquatics and fitness centres: 12
- Number of municipal golf courses: 8
- Number of outdoor municipal swimming pools: 8
- Number of wading pools: 7
- Number of indoor arenas: 18
- Number of tennis courts: 161

Source: City of Calgary

COLLABORATIVE GARDENING

Calgary's Horticultural Society operate a series of 15 community gardens, available for anyone interested in gardening but in need of earth to dig in. Designed to beautify neighbourhoods, promote camaraderie and facilitate environmental awareness, these gardens are available for a nominal rent. Most of these gardens, the smallest of which contain six plots, are earmarked for food, with smaller sections devoted to flowers. Gardeners are expected to participate in spring and fall clean-ups and to maintain their own plots and garden common areas throughout the growing season.

Source: Calgary Horticultural Society.

NOSE HILL

Nose Hill Park is one of the largest urban parks in Canada. Covering 11.27 km^2, the park is home to a host of wildlife, including 136 species of birds. It is also the highest point in the city limits, offering spectacular views of the Rocky Mountains and the prairies. Mule deer and white-tailed deer have also been spotted grazing on the abundant shrubs. Coyotes frequent the park and dog owners are wary — skir-

Did you know...

that Calgarians recycle 31,000 Christmas trees annually?

mishes between the wild animals and dogs have been widely reported.

More than 300 km of informal trails have been developed by bird watchers, mountain bikers and nature enthusiasts. The city of Calgary estimates that thousands of people use the park daily and has begun construction on a paved pathway system designed to reduce damage caused by heavy human traffic.

The Grand

Perched on the corner of 1st Street and 6th Ave. SW, the Grand Theatre reopened with much fanfare in the spring of 2006 after decades of being used for golf driving ranges and movie theatres.

Under the management of Theatre Junction, the building was rescued from certain demolition when the group campaigned to raise $12 million to purchase the Grand.

In the early 19th century, it attracted stars from Vaudeville and beyond, with Sarah Bernhardt making a rare appearance. Fred Astaire also brought his magical feet to the stage.

Despite its successes, the theatre has also had its share of controversy. When high profile manager/promoter William Sherman sold advertising on the fire curtains, upper crust patrons sniffed at the audacity of gaudy advertising in their opulent art house.

The massive renovations that began in 2004 resulted in a fusion of modern and historic design, with exposed bricks and chandeliers. The new theatre boasts 50-foot ceilings and modern lighting and technology. The second floor lounge is complimented by distinctive restrooms, with unisex hand wash sinks behind pink opaque glass. A circular cutout from the second floor acts as a portal to what's happening on the main floor, which houses a fashionable restaurant and bar.

A state of the art lighting grid allows technicians to cater to any form of production. Using movable seating, up to eight different formations can be created.

Did you know...

COMMUNITY TIES

Calgary has 186 communities and neighbourhoods, many of which have opened old doors and created new ones to receive some of the city's latest arrivals. In 2006, the populations of twelve of the city's communities increased by more than 1,000, including Tuscany, Evergreen and Panorama Hills. Four neighbourhoods more than doubled their populations, including Manchester, Alyth/Bonnybrook and Auburn Bay, which grew by 5450 percent!

IF HE BUILDS IT

One of Calgary's most well-known sons was Maxwell Bates. A writer, poet and painter, Bates was also a respected architect who trained under and worked with his father, William Stanley Bates. The duo contributed much to Calgary's architecture. Bates senior designed the Grain Exchange and Burns buildings, and Bates Junior worked on the Allied Arts Centre and private residences throughout the city.

These contributions were important to Calgary's cityscape, but Maxwell's architectural career was best defined by his ecclesiastical designs, which include the impressive, neo-gothic St. Mary's Cathedral. The Cathedral — officially the Cathedral of the Immaculate Conception of the Blessed Virgin Mary — was originally dedicated in 1889 and redesigned by Bates and reopened in 1957,

Did you know...

after nearly three decades of planning and fundraising. From sod to ceiling, the entire church was resurrected, with nothing saved from the original church except the four bells that continue to ring in the building's belfry.

C.O.P.

Canada Olympic Park, operated by CODA (the Canada Olympic Development Association) is a legacy of the 1988 Olympic winter games. The facilities are used both for athletic training and for recreational purposes.

For the winter sports enthusiasts, the park is used for skiing and snowboarding; in the summer, it is used for cycling (there are 25 km of bike trails) and hiking. The park is also a venue for many summer concerts and festivals.

RATS!

The Norway Rat is one of the most destructive animals known to humans. They contaminate food, spread disease and their incessant tunneling can destabilize sewer and water lines, streets and even buildings.

Calgary is, therefore, blessed not to have a rat problem. This is not by luck. The province has had a strident "anti-rat" program in place for decades. In 1950, rats were first reported along Alberta's eastern border. But rodent cries of "Go west, young rat!" were silenced by strident rat control initiatives, including massive poisoning campaigns. Public education has also figured prominently in Alberta's successful war against rats. Every Albertan is responsible for keeping the rodent out. Under law, only research labs can have rats in Alberta and it is illegal for private citizens to keep white rats, hooded rats or any of the strains of domesticated Norway rats. Violators face a fine of $5,000.

Source: Alberta Government.

DWELLINGS BY THE NUMBERS
- Total number of housing units in the Calgary municipality: 356,375
- Percentage that are single detached homes: 61.4
- Percentage that are row houses: 8.9
- Percentage that are semi-detached houses: 6.1
- Percentage that are apartments/others: 23.6
- 70.6 percent of Calgarians own their homes, 29.4 percent rent.

Source: Canadian Mortgage and Housing Corporation.

THIS OLD HOUSE
A total of 76 percent of Calgary's homes were built before 1991, with about 5.5 percent preceding 1946. The remaining 24 percent were built since 1991.

Source: Statistics Canada.

CHINATOWN
In the heart of Calgary's downtown, what was once a mere handful of Chinese businesses is now a bona fide Chinatown. Indeed, it is the third largest Chinatown in Canada. Spanning six blocks and covering one-twentieth of the entire downtown, the streets of Chinatown bustle day and night, seven days a week.

While only six percent of Calgary's population is Chinese, Calgary's Chinese Cultural Centre — a huge draw that attracts a quarter of a million visitors each year — is the largest facility of its kind in North America.

Opened in 1992, the centre is home to a Chinese library, a museum, a Chinese school, a gymnasium and a gift store. Modeled after the Hall of Prayers of the Temple of Heaven near the Forbidden City in Beijing, the Centre's blue-glazed roof tiles, traditional woodwork and ornate painting give visitors an awe-inspiring glimpse into classical China without leaving the modern western Canadian city of Calgary.

Not all is grandeur and gaiety in Calgary's Chinatown. It, like other North American Chinatowns, is also home to some of the city's poorest people. The average annual household income in Chinatown in 2000 was just over $16,000, compared to an average of nearly $58,000 for Calgary as a whole. This means that an astonishing 57 percent of Chinatown's 1,200 residents lived in low-income households.

Weblinks

Fish Creek Provincial Park
www.cd.gov.ab.ca/enjoying_alberta/parks/featured/fishcreek/index.asp
Online home of Fish Creek Provincial Park in Calgary, where visitors can see nature up close and personal.

Devonian Gardens
www.calgary.ca/docgallery/bu/parks_operations/devonian_self_guide.pdf
Online brochure for Calgary's Devonian Gardens — not to be confused with Edmonton's gardens of the same name! Find out more about this urban oasis, one of the world's largest indoor parks.

Calgary Zoo
www.calgaryzoo.org
Check out this site to see what's to see as well as what's happening at the world renowned Calgary Zoo.

Calgary's Architecture: Glass, Steel and Stone
www.glasssteelandstone.com/ByCityResults/Canada/Calgary.php
Check out this website for features on some important architectural feats in Calgary.

Weather

Calgary weather climate is influenced by two factors — its elevation of 1,128 m above sea level and its proximity to the Rocky Mountains. The Rockies create a barrier to weather patterns coming from the west, in particular the Pacific Ocean. This means that Calgary experiences a mostly moderate climate, is semi-arid with low to moderate amounts of precipitation.

Calgary is the sunniest major city in the country and the city is well known for its fair weather. Temperatures are capable of enormous swings. Warm Chinook winds can send winter temperatures up to 20°C, while summer time evening temperatures go down dramatically.

As in most Canadian cities, winter is winter, and it takes a hearty soul to enjoy the -11°C average temperature from December to February. But unlike other Canadian cities, Calgarians find respite from the January deep freezes thanks to Chinook winds.

DAILY AVERAGE TEMPERATURES (°C)

Jan	Feb	Mar	Apr	May	Jun	Jul	Aug	Sep	Oct	Nov	Dec
-8.9	-6.1	-1.9	4.6	9.8	13.8	16.2	15.6	10.8	5.4	-3.1	-7.4

Source: Environment Canada.

They Said It

AND THE WINNER IS . . .

- Record High: 36.1°C on July 15, 1919
- Record Low: -45°C on February 4, 1893
- Record Rainfall (in a day): 95.3 mm on July 15, 1927
- Record Snowfall (in a day): 48.4 cm on May 6, 1981
- Record Wind Speed (maximum hourly speed km/h): 105 km/h, on April 13, 1935
- Record Wind Gust: 127km/h, on June 10, 1956 and January 27, 1976
- Record Wind Chill: -55.1°C, on December 15, 1964
- Record Humidex: 36.9°C, on July 13, 2002
- Record Hours of Sunshine: 16.2 hours of sunshine, on June 26, 1973

Source: Environment Canada.

SUN CITY

Calgary comes in first place for the most sunshine among Canadian cities. The city enjoys 332.93 days of sunshine each year. Medicine Hat, at 329.88 sunshine days, comes second. By comparison, Winnipeg sees 317.78 sunny days, Victoria, 306.27, Montréal, 303.48, Toronto, 302.85, Halifax, 290.17, and St. John's, just 270.38 sunny days.

Calgarians enjoy the sun most in the winter. With an average 366.21 hours of sunshine in December, January and February, Calgary edges out it's nearest competitor, Winnipeg, which logs an average 358.24 hours of winter sunshine. Compare this to Chilliwack, the Canadian city with the 100th sunniest winter with just 72.05 hours of sunshine.

Pleasant autumns earn the city second place honors, at 512.08 hours of sun in September, October and November. Only Medicine Hat is sunnier in the autumn months.

Take 5 DAVID SPENCE'S TOP FIVE
INFLUENTIAL WEATHER EVENTS IN CALGARY

Besides forecasting Calgary's weather, David Spence likes to get out and enjoy the abundant sunshine and the famous Chinooks. He and his family can often be found in the many campgrounds and hiking trails of the foothills and the Rocky Mountains.

1. **Warm Winter Olympics:** Calgary was basking in the world spotlight in February of 1988, hosting the Olympic Winter Games, and temperatures were spectacularly warm. We made 18 degrees on February 26th.

2. **My first ultra-warm Chinook:** I washed my car outside in the driveway when it hit 15 degrees on February 24, 1983. I had experienced nothing quite like it growing up in Winnipeg.

3. **St. Patrick's Day Snowstorm March 17, 1998:** Calgary rarely gets shut down by snowstorms, but this one paralyzed the city with 38 cm of snow falling during the storm. Somehow, I was able to drive to work. The station sent people out in four-wheel-drive vehicles to pick up employees to bring them to work.

4. **The July 28, 1981 Hailstorm:** To date, it was Calgary's most expensive weather disaster, causing $125 million in damage with hail the size of softballs. I was in Banff that day, and drove home in a company vehicle to find the Trans Canada highway lined with so much hail that it looked like snow. My own car was sitting in an outdoor parking lot, and was written off due to the damage.

5. **The September 7, 1991 Hailstorm:** It surpassed the storm from ten years earlier — with more than $300 million in damage. Just as in the previous storm, I wasn't working that day, and got to enjoy the storm by watching it out the window. This time, though, my car was safely parked under a roof.

They Said It

CHINOOK WIND

Chinook winds are a unique feature of Calgary's weather. Said to mean 'snow eater' in the language of the Chinook First Nation tribe, these warm winds originate along the temperate Pacific ocean and blow down the lee-side of the Rocky Mountains, across the foothills to Calgary.

The temperate spike created by a Chinook can be as extreme as a 30°C increase. Usually, however, a Chinook raises temperatures by 12 to 15°C. Winter Chinooks are known to melt snow cover in less than a day.

Source: University of Alberta.

PRECIPITATION

The 412.6 mm of precipitation that Calgary receives each year is six times less than Prince Rupert's first place 2593.60 mm of precipitation, but is more than Canada's driest city, Whitehorse, which gets 267.40 mm.

RAIN

Calgary gets an average 320.6 mm of rain per year, only slightly below the Canadian average of 354.24 mm. On average, Canadians don a raincoat 145.44 days a year; Calgarians, however, will only need to 68 days a year.

Source: Environment Canada

WHEN THE BOW AND ELBOW FLOOD

Most of the time, the Elbow and Bow rivers wind peacefully through the city. But when conditions are right, both rivers are known to crest their banks, bringing devastation to the city.

 **FIVE CALGARY WEATHER TERMS**

1. **Chinooks:** Winds that occur when a mountain range is exposed to a strong prevailing crosswind; moist air is removed and the descending air then becomes warmer and drier as it is forced down the leeward side of the mountains.

2. **Foehn:** The relatively warm, dry gusty winds that occasionally occur to the leeward side of mountain ranges.

3. **Prairie Whitewasher:** A spring snowstorm.

4. **Hailstorm Alley:** An area on the high plains immediately east of the Rocky Mountains where the most frequent hailstorms in North America occur.

5. **Graupel:** A type of precipitation that consists of a snow crystal and a raindrop frozen together. Also called snow pellets.

Since 1897, the Bow River has flooded nine times, but only once since 1933. The Elbow has flooded 12 times since 1908.

June 2005 was the wettest month on record in Calgary history. Two hundred and forty-eight mm of rain fell on Calgary — more than three times the monthly average. As rain fell, water levels in the Bow and Elbow Rivers rose, flooding basements, washing out roads and taking out bridges for the first time since 1932.

In all, 1,500 Calgarians were evacuated, and 40,000 homes (1 in 10) were damaged. The flood cost $400 million, including $275 million in insured losses — making it one of the costliest natural disasters in Alberta's history.

They Said It

SNOWFALL

Calgary gets an average 126.67 cm of snow a year, earning 69th place in terms of snowfall in 100 Canadian cities. The snowiest Canadian city is Gander, NL, which is socked by an annual 443.13 cm of snow.

Thirty percent of Calgary's precipitation falls as snow. Calgary sees snowfall on 56.8 days a year. The city, however, only has snowfalls of 10 cm or more on 1.72 days a year and snowfalls of 25 cm or more on just .07 days. Calgarians can expect to have snow on the ground 88.39 days a year.

Source: Environment Canada

Snowfall has been recorded in Calgary in every month of the year. Check out these dates of record snowfalls.

January 3, 1913	25.4 cm
February, 1951	27.7 cm
March 13, 1889	24.1 cm
April 21, 1932	45.7 cm
May 6, 1981	48.4 cm
June 6, 1951	24.9 cm
July 23, 1918	0.3 cm
August 25, 1900	6.1 cm
September 19, 1895	22.9 cm
October 4, 1914	29.7 cm
November 13, 1914	35.6 cm
December 11, 1889	21.8 cm

Source: Environment Canada.

They Said It

"The country is one of pleasant temperatures with very little snowfall. Sleighs are seldom, if ever, used in Southern Alberta."
– A Canadian Pacific Railway promotional brochure

WARMEST WINTER OLYMPICS

When Calgary hosted the Olympic Winter Games in February 1988, the weather was, at times, anything but wintry. On February 26th Miami's high temperature of 19.4°C was only slightly warmer than Calgary's maximum for that day, an amazing 18.1°C. High temperatures were not the only weather-related story of the Games; high winds up to 100 km/h also wreaked havoc with event schedules. In all, 33 events had to be rescheduled.

Source: Environment Canada; CBC.

FREAKY WEATHER

The spring and summer season of 2003 was a short one thanks to freak storms. A dumping of 80 cm in April was followed by a May that saw snow on eight days. That spring, more than a metre of snow fell on the city.

While spring was late thanks to snow, fall was also cut short when, on September 16th, three cm fell thanks to temperatures that were 17 degrees cooler than normal. Lest one think there is a predictable pattern to Calgary's weather, it's worth remembering that on January 7th of that year, Calgary's mercury reached 17.6°C, the warmest January day in the city's history.

Source: Environment Canada.

Did you know...

that the annual expenditure for the city of Calgary to maintain the 12,000 km of roads with sanding, salting, plowing and snow removal is $17,000,000?

They Said It

"Gardening is indeed a challenge for the majority of gardeners on much of this vast continent, but southern Alberta takes the cake when it comes to an inhospitable climate for gardening, what with Chinooks, winter dehydration, and a short growing season."

– Horticulturalist David Tarrant

DREAMING OF A WHITE CHRISTMAS

Of all Canadian cities, Calgary has among the lowest chance of a white Christmas — just a 59 percent chance. The probability of having a "perfect Christmas" (defined as one with at least two cm on the ground and snow in the air) is even lower at four percent. The greatest snowfall recorded on a Christmas day in Calgary was the 10.2 cm that fell on December 25th, 1923.

Source: Environment Canada

SNOW JOB

Calgarians are responsible for cleaning up after storms. Street bylaw 20M88 requires residents to remove snow and ice from any sidewalk adjacent to their property within 24 hours of the snow or ice being deposited. Failure to clear sidewalks will result in a warning notice, a ticket, or the offending resident will be compelled to pick up the tab for the city's clearing of the area of snow and ice.

THE ALLEY

The telltale sound of stones pinging off the roofs in Calgary is all too familiar. Calgary is situated in an area known as 'Hail Alley.'

On September 7th, 1991, a suppertime storm that lasted 30 minutes

Did you know...

that of the biggest dumps of 25 cm (or more) of snow that fell in Calgary over the last 120 years, only one occurred in January while six were in May?

Take 5 CALGARY'S FIVE HOTTEST DAYS
(AS RECORDED AT THE AIRPORT)

1. **July 15, 1919:** 36.1°C
2. **July 25, 1933:** 36.1°C
3. **August 3, 1914:** 35.6°C
4. **June 26, 1926:** 35.6°C
5. **September 1, 1967:** 33.3°C

Source: Environment Canada.

dropped 10 cm diameter hail on Calgary, turning trees into firewood, breaking windows and siding and crushing birds. Homeowners filed a record 116,000 insurance claims, with property damage losses exceeding $300 million. This was Canada's most destructive hailstorm and the second most costly storm.

Source: Environment Canada

MORE STORMY WEATHER
Calgary averages 27.35 days per year of lightning earning a fifth place spot for Canadian cities. Windsor, ON, ranks first with 33.24 days of lightning.

Source: Environment Canada.

GREATEST OUTDOOR SHOW ON EARTH MUST GO ON
When you're playing host to the Greatest Outdoor Show on Earth, you can't let a little thing like the weather get in the way. Although Calgary's summers are generally pleasant, the weather has at times challenged event organizers.

In 1998, Stampede organizers had to contend with thunderstorms

Did you know...

that when Calgary was pounded by a severe hailstorm on July 16, 1996, the city's children made the best of it, donning mittens to make 'hailmen' and enjoying some rare summer sledding?

Take 5 — CALGARY'S FIVE COLDEST DAYS
(AS RECORDED AT THE AIRPORT)

1. **February 4, 1893:** - 45.0 °C
2. **January 31, 1893:** -44.4°C
3. **December 17,1924:** -42.8°C
4. **March 9 1951:** -37.2°C
5. **November 30, 1893:** -35°C

Source: Environment Canada.

on eight of the first ten days in July, prime Stampede time. July 4th brought a record-breaking 43 mm of rain, which fell in just six hours. That year it even rained on the Stampede breakfast.

In 1999, woolen caps and long johns replaced stetsons and chaps as unseasonably cold weather with temperatures hovering around the zero mark had visitors shivering in their cowboy boots.

GROWING SEASON

Calgary gets 169 frost-free days per year on average. Some of them occur in the fall and even winter because of the Chinook factor. Those winter thaws are not counted in the growing season statistics, so normally there is about 115 consecutive frost-free days per season, usually occurring between May 23rd and September 15th.

Did you know...

that on March 22nd, 1968, Calgary experienced the lowest relative humidity ever recorded in Canada, at 6 percent?

Did you know...

that on average Alberta may experience up to 30 Chinook days per year? There has only been one winter month in the last 100 years that has not had a thaw.

WITHER THE LUCK O' THE IRISH?

The luck of the Irish was nowhere to be found in March 1998. Mother Nature ensured that nothing would be green on that St. Patrick's Day as the city endured its worst March snowstorm in 113 years.

The airport recorded 32 cm of snow, but most other parts of the city received 40 to 45 cm. The downtown core was completely abandoned when the transit system was forced to shut down. Nary a leprechaun could be spotted. For the first time ever, St. Patrick's Day celebrations in the city were cancelled.

WIND

Calgary scores 29th of Canadian cities when it comes to wind speeds. Winds blow at an average 14.8km/h. Compare this to St. John's, NL, the windiest Canadian city, where wind speeds average 23.3km/h, and Kelowna, BC, which has the calmest winds blowing at an average 5.38km/h.

Weblinks

Weather Winners
www.on.ec.gc.ca/weather/winners/intro-e.html
Find out how Calgary ranks in 72 different weather categories at the Environment Canada Website.

The Flood of '05
www.calgaryarea.com/calgary_flood.htm
Checkout this website for some photos of the infamous Calgary flood of '05.

Calgary Cams
http://65.104.36.247/default.asp?display=cams&area=calgary&TextOnly=
See for yourself what the weather is like in Calgary with this page linking you to live feeds of a series of strategically placed city cameras.

Crime and Punishment

CRIMELINE

1875: Fort Calgary is established by the North West Mounted Police.

1884: In February, murderer Jess Williams is tried and convicted in Calgary. He becomes the first non-Native hanged in the Northwest Territories.

1885: The Calgary Police Service is established.

1889: William "Jumbo" Fisk is charged with killing Rosalie New Grass, a Cree woman. Racism rears its head and in a first trial Fisk is found not guilty. A second trial rights the first — sort of. Fisk is found guilty of manslaughter.

1902: A man known only as 'Scouten' is arrested for the shooting death of Arthur Simpson at the Atlantic Hotel. He was found hiding in a horse stable after being on the lam for three days.

1903: On December 10th, convicted murderer Ernest Cashel escapes from jail where he was held on charges of robbing and killing a rancher and sentenced to hang December 15th. After a 46-day manhunt he was recaptured.

1904: On February 2nd, recaptured fugitive Ernest Cashel is hanged for murder, becoming the first man to be hanged in Calgary.

1912: John C. Davis shoots his wife Minnie Dixon along with the private detective he hired to track her down. He then turns the gun on himself. It's later discovered that Davis' real name is Spencer Holder and he had deserted a wife and two children in Alabama.

1914: Jasper Collins is the last person to be publicly hanged in Calgary. His crime is murder, his victim, a lawyer.

1917: On July 2nd, 39-year-old Constable Arthur Duncan is the first Calgary police officer to die in the line of duty. His killer was never found.

1923: Calgarian Filumena Losandro becomes one of few women to be hanged in Canada. She is 22 when sent to the gallows.

1928: Calgary police report an increased incidence in joy riding as young people enjoy their cars — too much.

1940: Military police have to quash a violent race riot between white soldiers and residents of Calgary's "Harlem Town" near the railway tracks east of downtown.

1941: An elevator agent for the Alberta Wheat Pool, Victor Ramberg, and his wife are found not guilty of murder after the mercy killing of their two-year-old son who was afflicted with optical nerve cancer.

1943: Vera Bell becomes the first woman to work for the Calgary Police Service, albeit on a temporary basis.

1946: Four Calgary police women are patrolling dance halls, streets and the city's rough spots, and assisting detectives on the morality beat.

Take 5 TOP FIVE CRIMES COMMITTED IN CALGARY

1. **Mischief offenses, including graffiti and other damage to property**
2. **Theft from vehicles**
3. **Break and enters, domestic and business**
4. **Assaults**
5. **Vehicle Thefts**

Source: Calgary Police Service.

1995: Dorothy Joudrie is charged with attempted murder after shooting her estranged husband, oil executive Earl Joudrie, at her home in Calgary. Joudrie was riddled with six bullets.

1995: On July 17th, Christine Silverberg is appointed chief of the Calgary Police Service. The 45-year-old becomes the first female police chief of a major Canadian city.

1995: Calgary gets its first police helicopter.

1996: Found to be suffering from mental illness, Dorothy Joudrie is acquitted of charges for attempted murder of her estranged husband, Earl.

1997: On March 26th, the Bre-X bubble bursts.

1999: Calgarian Catherine Tkachuck is the first woman in Canada to be convicted of double first-degree murder for the brutal killing of her adoptive parents.

2001: On October 17th, Constable Darren Beatty was fatally injured in the line of duty. He becomes the 11th member of the Calgary Police Service to die on the job.

CALGARIAN CASUALTIES IN THE LINE OF DUTY

- 1917 - Constable Arthur Duncan (shot in jaw and chest)
- 1933 - Inspector Joe Carruthers (shot in chest)
- 1941 - Constable Wilf Cox (motorcycle accident)
- 1957 - Constable Ken Delmage (motorcycle collision with vehicle)
- 1974 - Detective Boyd Davidson (shot in neck)
- 1976 - Staff Sgt. Keith Harrison (shot in stomach)
- 1977 - Constable Bill Shelever (shot in head)
- 1992 - Constable Rob Vanderwiel (shot in neck)
- 1993 - Constable Rick Sonnenberg (hit while attempting to stop stolen vehicle)
- 2000 - Constable John Petropoulos (injuries sustained in fall)
- 2001 - Constable Darren Beatty (injuries sustained during training exercise)

CALGARY PI

Arriving in Calgary in 1919 with his wife and three children, Louis Leonoff opened Calgary's first private detective agency. A franchise of the MacDonald Detective Agency in Winnipeg, the office was situated in the old *Calgary Herald* newspaper building. His biggest customers were insurance companies growing increasingly suspicious of fraudulent claims.

CALGARY CRIME BY THE NUMBERS (2005)

- Number of recorded homicides: 39
- Sex crimes: 801
- Assaults: 6,729
- Robberies: 1,186
- Total attacks against property (break and enter, vehicle theft and fraud): 52,805
- Impaired driving charges: 3,571
- Dangerous driving charges: 164
- Number of fatal motor vehicle collisions: 37
- Nonfatal motor vehicle collisions: 3,555
- Parking lot nonfatal injury collisions: 158

Calgary's Jack the Ripper

In 1889, Calgary was in the midst of an economic boom. Good times attracted all manner of characters, among them a 32-year-old blacksmith from Ontario. William "Jumbo" Fisk was a tough guy, having fought for government forces in the Riel Rebellion where he lost a finger in the battle of Frog Lake. Earning the nickname Jumbo (after the elephant of P.T. Barnum's three ring circus), the girthful Fisk arrived in Calgary with a taste for liquor, women and gambling.

In his new city, Fisk became co-owner of the seedy Turf Club and he soon became acquainted with the wrong side of the law, facing several arrests for public drunkenness and earning a reputation as a liquor trafficker. In 1889, murder was added to his rap sheet.

Like all people in Canada, Calgarians were, in 1889, mesmerized by stories of another murderer, the rampage of London's infamous Jack the Ripper. The Fisk case was chillingly familiar to the far-off Ripper saga, and Calgarians were enthralled.

Fisk's victim was a young Cree woman, Rosalie New Grass. Part of a small, poor Cree community living on Calgary's outskirts, Rosalie earned a meager and dangerous living working as a prostitute. On the night of her death, Fisk admitted to taking Rosalie to an upstairs room of the Turf Club for "immoral purposes."

That same evening, her mutilated, blood-soaked body was discovered. Fisk's professions of his innocence faced strong evidence to the contrary. A friend of Fisk's testified that Fisk had borrowed a dollar to take the woman upstairs. This friend also told the coroner's inquest how he locked the door after hearing loud groaning noises. Half an hour later, when he returned to let Fisk out, he noticed Fisk's cheek was covered in blood and New Grass was sprawled on the bed, covered in blood and near death. Rather than seek help, the two men went for drinks, leaving her to die.

TRAFFIC VIOLATIONS
- Total number of speeding tickets issued: 231,061
- Running a red light: 14,798
- Total number of traffic summonses: 376,895

Source: Calgary Police Service.

Advice To Young Men

Ernest Cashel was one of Calgary's most notorious fugitives. The young man began stealing at the age of 14 and was perpetually on the wrong side of the law ever after. He first arrived in Calgary intending to open a barber shop, but when that failed he started forging cheques. When a warrant was issued for his arrest, he fled the city.

Calgary police chief Thomas English soon caught up to Cashel , whosurrendered without a struggle and they were soon aboard a train for Calgary. On their journey back, Cashel's leg irons were removed so he could eat his dinner, but before dessert Cashel was a free man. On a visit to the men's room, Cashel took his leave from a window of the moving locomotive.

This would prove to be a turning point in the young con's life. Shortly after Cashel vanished, a local rancher named Isaac Belt went missing and neighbours suspected foul play. Thinking that Cashel was somehow involved, a special constable was assigned to his case.

While on the lam, Cashel started using a number of aliases. When he brazenly returned to Calgary as "Nick Carter," he convinced two young men to procure ammunition and clean clothes for him. He also visited a local rancher from whom he borrowed a horse, ostensibly to round up his own steed. When he didn't return the rancher's ride, the rancher contacted police, but not before Cashel had broken into the home of a woman and stole a diamond ring.

On January 24, 1903, the long arm of the law again caught up with Ernest Cashel. When he was arrested, he was wearing the cor-

STOLEN CARS

Calgary is an auto theft hotspot, with 753 cars stolen per 100,000 population. By contrast, Edmonton records 484 cars per 100,000 people stolen annually. Calgary has the 6th highest rate of auto thefts of all major Canadian cities.

Source: Canadian Direct Insurance.

duroy pants of the missing rancher Isaac Belt. In the absence of Belt's body, they could not charge him with murder. For theft and forgery, he was sentenced to three years of hard labour at the Stony Mountain Penitentiary in Manitoba.

In July, however, Belt's body was found floating in the Red Deer River and the 44-calibre bullet taken from the dead man's chest matched Cashel's gun. Cashel was found guilty and sentenced to hang on December 5th, 1903.

Wild stories began to circulate that American mobsters were en route to Calgary to spring the fugitive from his cell. While these rumours proved unfounded, the story was not yet over. When Cashel's brother John visited the prison, he slipped his incarcerated kin two revolvers. Later, Cashel's guards found themselves staring down the barrels of Cashel's guns. Cashel did it again. What happened next was the story of "the greatest manhunt in the history of the territories."

Cashel managed to elude the authorities for 45 days before they found him holed up in the basement of a farmhouse seven miles east of Calgary. After a standoff, the police threatened to burn him out and he surrendered. Punishment was swift. Ernest Cashel, just 21 years old, was hanged nine days later on February 2, 1904. He left behind a cautionary note which he titled "Advice to young men." His advice was pointed: "Stay at home, shun novels, bad company and cigarettes" and "Don't do anything, boys, you are afraid to let your mother know."

Take 5 TOP FIVE VEHICLES OF CHOICE FOR CALGARY CAR THIEVES

1. Chevrolet/GMC trucks
2. Honda Civic
3. Plymouth/Dodge van
4. Ford Truck
5. Dodge Truck

Source: Calgary Police Service.

BLACK FRIDAY

Once Phillipe Gagnon's glue-sniffing addiction spiraled out of control, his behavior became increasingly erratic and violent. On December 20th, 1974, frustrated after being refused his usual supply at a local market, he threatened the owner who immediately phoned the police.

Upon arriving at Gagnon's home the two responding police officers were greeted with gunfire and called for backup. Shortly after the other officers arrived, Gagnon fired, killing officer Boyd Harrison. The bullet splintered on impact, injuring six other cops.

The threat to the community prompted the police to evacuate the neighbourhood of Ramsey and to bring in a tank from the local military base. When they began leveling his ramshackle home, Gagnon ran out, pistols blazing, and met his end in a shower of bullets.

POLICING CALGARY

In 2005, there were 642 citizens per one Calgary Police Service officer (compared to 523 officers per 100,000 population in Toronto)
• Gross Expenditures for 2005: $226,565,000

Did you know...

That 92 percent of Calgarians are either "very satisfied" or "satisfied" with the service from the Calgary Police Service?

They Said It

> *"To optimize public safety in the City of Calgary."*
> **– the Mission Statement of the Calgary Police Service**

- Per capita cost: $237
- The total number of staff with the CPS: 2,111 (2005)
- There are 765 cars, vans, motorcycles and trucks in the CPS fleet
- The average wait time for priority calls to CPS: 6.1 minutes

Bio THE CLOWN PRINCE

An outspoken Irish immigrant with a penchant for the dramatic and the humorous, Paddy Nolan quickly rose to notoriety as a Calgary legal eagle with flair. He often used comedy to diffuse courtroom tension, even during the murder trial of Ernest Cashel. His wit was particularly evident in his frequent representation of Caroline "Mother" Fulham, one of Calgary's most colourful characters.

Nolan was a proud Irishman. He claimed to have been born on St. Patrick's day but, in truth, he came into the world a little too early — March 3rd, 1862. Nolan left his homeland after being kicked out of the Dublin University Philosophical Society for disruptive behavior. Departing on something of a whim, Nolan boarded a ship for Toronto by way of New York. Somehow he found his way to Calgary where he became the ninth lawyer to be issued a license by the territories.

Ever a booster of his adopted hometown, he once predicted of Calgary "it's going to be bigger than Dublin one day," even though its population was less than 4,000 at the time.

Nolan also expressed his wit and levity publicly to Calgarians. He was an amateur actor in Gilbert and Sullivan operettas and he shared his Irish witticisms in columns he wrote for the *Calgary Herald* between 1905-06. Paddy Nolan died suddenly in 1913 at the age of 50.

Take 5   TOP FIVE DISPATCHED CALLS
IN 2005

1. **To check on welfare of individuals** (23,011 calls)
2. **Alarms** (14,202 calls)
3. **Suspicious persons** (13,188 calls)
4. **Domestic** (11,603 calls)
5. **Theft** (11,042 calls)

- Number of Calgary Police Service community stations and district offices: 368

SALARY

The Calgary Police Service pay scale is competitive with other Canadian police services. The following is a breakdown of the salary range for the rank of constable. A constable's pay class increases on their anniversary date during the first five years of service.

Class Annually 2007

5th Class Constable	$ 49,662.12
4th Class Constable	$ 52,541.08
3rd Class Constable	$ 61,177.97
2nd Class Constable	$ 66,935.89
1st Class Constable	$ 71,974.08

TAKING A BIG BITE OUT OF CALGARY CRIME

Since Crime Stoppers came to Calgary in 1982, they have received 43,108 tips leading to 5,046 arrests. They have also been instrumental

Did you know...

that on average, 13 cars are stolen each day in Calgary?

in recovering $13,033,443 worth of stolen property. Their reward program has also authorized $997,725 to tipsters. In October of 2006, their hotline tips led to the seizure of $3,911,510 of illegal drugs.

Source: Crimestoppers.

Pig Farmer and Hell Raiser

In the early part of the 1900's, it was acceptable for the men of Calgary to belly up to any one of the growing number of taverns. Not so for a woman, except for Caroline "Mother" Fulham, a stout pig farmer with a sharp tongue and quick wit.

Fulham was a constant thorn in the side of the city's police force and the more genteel citizens of downtown Calgary. She kept pigs in her backyard and often took garbage from hotels and restaurants to supply slop to her animals, a practice that earned her the nickname "The Queen of Garbage Row." It was during one of her slop-seeking excursions that Fulham was punched by staff of the Alberta Hotel.

Her assault led to a trial that attracted so many curious onlookers, it had to be moved to the town hall to accommodate everyone. Represented by notoriously funny lawyer Paddy Nolan, Fulham entertained the crowd with her bravado and cheeky remarks directed at the judge.

Later she would sue the Canadian Pacific Railway (CPR) after one of their trains killed one of her wayward cows.

Perhaps the one incident that made her most famous involved a concerned doctor who stopped her after noticing she was favouring one leg. When she rolled down her leggings, the shocked physician said, "I'll bet a dollar there's not another leg in Calgary as dirty as that." She responded by rolling down her other stocking, exposing the other leg and promptly took the man's dollar.

GATHERED FROM THE 2005 CALGARY POLICE SERVICE CITIZEN SURVEY

1. **Illegal gang activity/organized crime**
2. **Drug law enforcement**
3. **Traffic violations** (speeding, unsafe driving)
4. **House break-ins** (break and enter)
5. **Violent youth crime**

FINE, THEN

- Fine for stopping on a crosswalk or failing to stop before entering a crosswalk or an intersection is $115.
- Fine for failing to yield to a pedestrian in a crosswalk or passing another vehicle stopped at a crosswalk is $575.
- If you're entering a driveway or alley you must yield to pedestrians. The fine for failing to stop before crossing the sidewalk when exiting a driveway or alley is $115.
- In urban areas drivers aren't allowed to back their vehicles into an intersection or over a crosswalk. The penalty for doing so is $115.
- Passing in playground zones and school zones: $172
- When an emergency vehicle is approaching or overtaking you, you must pull over to the nearest curb and stop, clear of any intersection. Failing to yield the right-of-way: $172

Did you know...

that the Calgary Health Region condemned 78 grow-op homes in 2003 and 2004?

Did you know...

that in 2005, over 700 volunteers clocked 66,348 hours with the Calgary Police Service?

- Fine for making an illegal "U" turn: $115.
- Fine for not wearing your seatbelt: $115.
- Fine for driving with your windows obscured by snow, frost, steam, dirt or any other material is $115.

Hoax of the Century

In 1993, shareholders in Calgary-based mining company Bre-X were delighted to learn the company had struck gold in Busang, Indonesia. This find, the largest ever, sent company stocks skyrocketing from less than $1 to more than $200.

The euphoria was short-lived. Soon, details of the company's shady inner workings began to surface. On March 26th, 1997, the miners tasked with extracting the high-priced ore reported there was little or no gold at the mine. Shares plummeted, sending ripples through the stock market. The Toronto Stock Exchange immediately halted trading of Bre-X stocks, while the company's executive and staff refused to respond to the barrage of media and shareholder questions.

Talk of a massive hoax reached fever pitch with company's chief geologist, Mike de Guzman, committing suicide by leaping out of a helicopter shortly before the announcement. The details of his death have been the topic of much media speculation. In true conspiracy theory fashion, others have speculated he is still alive and well, hiding in the jungle. Adding fuel to this saga is the fact that his badly decomposed body was never tested against dental records and the $30,000 he was allegedly carrying was never recovered.

The debacle cost investors billions, with estimates varying from $3 to $6 billion. To date, no one has served jail time for the Bre-X hoax. David Walsh, the founder of the company who made $84 million selling Bre-X stock, died in 1998. The only person facing civil charges, chief geologist John Felderhof, lives in the Cayman Islands. His trial has been repeatedly delayed due to legal loopholes.

Take 5 FIVE STRAIGHT UP FACTS ON GANG MEMBERS IN CALGARY FROM THE CALGARY POLICE SERVICE

1. Age that gangs begin recruiting for new members: 12
2. Average age of gang members killed in Calgary: 20
3. Percentage of gang members that are victims of violence compared to a regular community member: 75
4. Percentage of 2005 Calgary homicides linked to gangs: 20
5. Percentage of gang members who are attacked or killed who know their attacker: 86

BIG BROTHER IS WATCHING

It's a sore spot for many Calgary drivers. Cameras mounted on traffic light standards clocking red light runners and sending out tickets. Dubbed red light cameras, they photograph vehicles entering the intersection after the light turns red.

Calgary is the only city in North America with portable red light cameras — they can be moved throughout the city. If you want to keep track of them check out the homepage of the Calgary Police Service — it posts the locations of red light cameras and photo radar across the city.

- Number of red light cameras: 36
- Number of red light camera ready intersections: 44

Source: Calgary Police Service.

Did you know...

that Calgary's Florence Filumena Losandro was one of few women to be hanged in Canada? Sent to the gallows at the age of 22 in 1923, the Calgary Opera created a tribute to the Italian immigrant tried for the murder of a constable in 2005, staging *Filumena* to packed audiences across Canada for Alberta's centennial celebrations.

Bio MADAME PEARL MILLER

One of Calgary's most notorious citizens, Pearl Miller was a madame with a reputation for providing discreet services to the upper crust of the city and for having an amicable relationship with law enforcement.

Miller moved to Calgary just before World War I and worked as a prostitute in the brothels along east side 6th Ave downtown, where she was arrested for vagrancy in 1914. In 1926, the entrepreneurial Miller opened her first brothel a convenient block from the King Eddy Hotel in East Calgary.

A wealthy client who remains a mystery helped her procure a huge house just south of the city limits. The home soon became the most famous brothel in Alberta. It was never raided and it attracted high-class clientele to its opulent drawing rooms.

Miller was known for euphemistically calling her business the "carriage trade." In 1913, her brash move to relocate to 19th St. SW, very close to swanky Mt. Royal, ruffled many feathers. In 1939, the police raided her establishment and charged her for a liquor violation. Six weeks later, the police knocked on her door, this time charging her with running a bawdy house. Miller paid a heavy fine and moved back to 9th Ave.

In 1941, she was raided again. This time she served a three-month prison sentence. In prison, she found religion and following her release she spent her remaining years attempting to educate young women on the perils of prostitution.

Pearl Miller died at the age of 57. Her Mt. Royal House is now a residential care centre. A Lunchbox Theatre staged a one-act musical in her honour named *Remember Pearl Miller* (loosely based on the John H. Gray 1971 book about her life.)

They Said It

HAWC1

HAWC1 is first Canadian municipal police helicopter. It lifted off for its first official patrol on July 16th, 1995. HAWC1 can respond to calls quickly, averaging only 90 seconds to get to any location.

Weblinks

The Calgary Police Service
http://www.gov.calgary.ab.ca/police/
The Calgary Police have an easy-to-navigate website with detailed information on local services, key messages and police station locations. Recent quarterly and annual reports chock full of information are also available for download.

Crime Stoppers, Calgary
www.calgarycrimestoppers.org/districtc.html
Crimestoppers is a grassroots campaign aiming to reduce the amount of crime on Calgary's streets through citizen involvement. The site features current statistics and bulletins displaying photos of alleged criminals.
Source: Crimestoppers.

Youthlink Calgary
www.youthlinkcalgary.com/index.php?id=32
An information-rich website devoted to educating youth and adults about the perils of crime.

Culture

Calgary culture is a mix of old and new. It draws heavily on its cowboy past and its oil patch identity, and is infused with the influences of a steady influx of people from around the world. From the Stampede to the newly-minted Grand theatre, from Arts Central to the Palomino Social Club, the city is giddy with promise and creative energy.

ARTISTS

Among large prairie cities, it is in Calgary where artists have the highest average earnings.

- Number of artists in Canada: 130,700, 0.8 percent of the workforce
- Number in Calgary : 4,457, 0.8 percent of the workforce
- Calgary artists' average earnings (2001): $21,500
- Gap between artists' earnings and overall workforce average: 42 percent

Calgary has:
- 335 actors
- 590 artisans and craftspersons
- 70 conductors, composers and arrangers
- 360 dancers

- 1,095 musicians and singers
- 170 other performers
- 525 painters, sculptors and other visual artists
- 545 producers, directors, choreographers and related artists
- 885 writers

Source: Canada Council for the Arts.

THE ARTS ORGANIZED

Before March 2005, Calgary didn't have an official arts authority. Calgary Arts Development Authority (CADA) was formed after the Civic Arts initiative was implemented by City Council. Acting as a mediator between the municipality and arts groups, CADA dispenses funding to artists in the city.

Did you know...

that Calgary is home to over 20 live theatre groups?

MUSICAL WONDER

The Globe and Mail declared the Calgary Folk Music Festival to be "one of the seven musical wonders of the world." The 2006 Festival was a sold-out event, featuring 65 artists from 15 countries on seven stages.

Featured artists included Kris Kristofferson, Macy Gray, Feist, Broken Social Scene, Ani DiFranco, Bedouin Soundclash, Dave Alvin and Dan Bern. New features included a secondary stage on Friday and Saturday night and Boot Camp, intensive master classes at Cantos Music Foundation.

Take 5 MATT MASTER'S TOP FIVE CALGARY AREA HONKYTONKS

Matt Masters is a proud Calgarian. A Country and Western singer and songwriter with an interest in local history, Matt gained recognition for his 2005 Alberta Centennial Tour when he took an Alberta Music History Revue to 100 communities around the province.

1. **A Bar Named Sue** – (410 4 St SW) A hole in the wall that takes you back in time. Sawdust on the floor and C&W every night.

2. **The Palomino Smokehouse** – (109 7th Ave SW) Good food, good music, good looking!

3. **The Ranchman's** – (9615 Macleod Trail South) The Ranchman's is a required stop when you and the honey have a falling out.

4. **The Stop** – (123 Government Road, Black Diamond) Hitch up here on your way down the Cowboy Trail. Southern Alberta's only authentic Chicken Toss.

5. **Broken City** – (613 11th Ave SW) Dancin' and drinkin' are the order of the day every day of the year. The music might not be pure country, but this is pure Calgary.

They Said It

ALL IN ORDER

- Calgarians who are recipients of the Order of Canada: 137
- Officers of the Order of Canada: 54
- Members of the Order of Canada: 80
- Companions of the Order: 3

CULTURAL SPENDING

In 2005, Canadians spent $25.1 billion on cultural goods and services.

Calgarians were among the highest cultural spenders in Canada. Indeed, the city ranked third among Canadian cities. In 2005, Calgarians spent a total of $1 billion on culture. Broken down, that means that each Calgarian spent $997 on cultural goods and services.

Calgarians also get a first place rating when it comes to buying art and paying to attend cultural events.

Source: Hill Strategies Research Inc.

Did you know...

That on November 28, 2006, Calgary city council voted in favour of increasing Calgary Arts Development's annual granting and programs budget by $502, 500 — approximately $0.50 per capita — to a total of $3,090,500.

ARTSHUB

A cluster of galleries and artists' studios, ArtCentral celebrated its second anniversary in October 2006.

Divided into 56 different spaces, the collective environment is an ideal place to catch a glimpse of works in progress as sculptures hone

Bio JANN ARDEN: SUCCESS ON HER OWN TERMS

"Where I am from is who I am," says Jann Arden. At the turn of the century her grandmother came up from Utah to southern Alberta and the family has been there ever since.

Arden literally burst onto the Canadian stage in 1994, winning two Junos. In the space of a year, the singer/songwriter went from a relative unknown making music in her basement apartment to one of Canada's biggest headline acts. She has been there ever since.

In 1995, Arden took home three more Junos, one each for Best Female Vocalist, Songwriter of the Year and Single of the Year for "Could I Be Your Girl." In 2001, she garnered another Best Female Artist award, then again in 2002 for Best Songwriter.

An outspoken comedian with a razor sharp wit, she has strong opinions about women and how they view their lives. It is that insight that has proved to be so powerful with her legion of fans and has helped her sell more than two million albums.

In addition to a relentless touring schedule, she pens a regular advice column for Chatelaine magazine. Arden also has a career as a visual artist, specializing in watercolour. Her paintings often fetch thousands of dollars. For a time she also co-owned with her brother a popular Calgary eatery, the Arden Diner on 17th Ave.

She has also begun to carve out an acting career, appearing on such shows as "Robson Arms" and "This Hour Has 22 Minutes." She has performed in the widely popular female-run touring production of the "Vagina Monologues".

Arden lives in a modest house on the outskirts of Calgary.

They Said It

their work and painters craft their canvasses with most of the studios being open for public viewing.

Featuring art that ranges from provocative and modern to distinctly classic, the galleries buzz with life on the first Thursday of the month as the music of local jazz musicians plays in the background and smartly dressed servers offer cupcakes to visitors.

Situated in the heart of Calgary's theatre and entertainment district, it also hosts high-energy events and funky fashion shows with everyone from art students to aldermen rubbing shoulders in the atrium.

AT THE MOVIES

Calgary is home to three independent movie houses: The Plaza, the Globe and the Uptown.

• Movie screens in Calgary and Airdire: 144

Source: City of Calgary; foundlocally.com; Statistics Canada.

BIG SKY

With breathtaking landscapes and highly skilled workers, Calgary has garnered a reputation in Hollywood as a place to film everything from westerns to weekly serials. From "Unforgiven" to "Brokeback Mountain," directors and producers have recognized the value of the distinctive backdrop. With skies that stretch on forever and the rolling foothills of the Rocky Mountains, increasing numbers of filmmakers have recognized that this is the place to shoot big pictures without big budgets. "Brokeback Mountain," which won the Oscar for best director, was filmed entirely around Calgary, Kananaskis and Fort Macleod. The Calgary International Film Festival has grown to the fourth largest in Canada, screening films from local darlings Gary Burns and more established directors such as Pedro Aldomovar.

Bio COWBOY ICON

If Cow Town needs a poet laureate, it doesn't need to look any further than singer, songwriter and rancher Ian Tyson. Tyson's life echoes the lyrics you'd expect in the musical genre first labeled "Country and Western" by *Billboard Magazine* in 1949.

Born in Victoria, BC, in 1933, Tyson experienced cowboy culture through books until, against his father's wishes, he started participating in small rodeos. The consummate cowboy, he strove to "make eight" until he shattered his leg after being thrown from a horse. It was while he was recovering from the injury that he started plucking a guitar. Before going 'west,' Tyson headed east to Toronto. There he met Sylvia Fricker. Together they formed the folk duo "Ian and Sylvia" and made their mark in the folk music scene of the 60s. In 1969, the performing couple married.

In the early 70s, Tyson had a five-year stint hosting his own show on the CBC before following the words of his own popular and oft covered song, "Four Strong Winds"; he thought he'd go out to Alberta. To pay for the spread of land he purchased in the foothills south of Calgary, Tyson performed regularly at the Ranchman's, where his legend could best be described as two-fisted — both at the bar, and when dealing with patrons who didn't like his music.

From his T-Bar-Y ranch Tyson has produced 11 albums including the classics "Cowboyography" in 1987 and 1999's "The Lost Herd." He remains a cultural touchstone of Calgary's cowboy roots.

THE BIZ OF SHOW BIZ

Calgary's film industry boasts 163 companies and employs 2,200 people. Over the past 10 years, employment in this sector has shot up by 37.5 percent.

Source: Calgary Economic Development.

MOVIE MONEY

In 2006, 21 major film projects were shot in the Calgary area, and contributed $118 million to the local economy. As well, Calgary Economic Development issued $143,000 worth of city permits for the makers of 66 film, television and digital media projects, up 34 percent over 2005.

Source: Calgary Economic Development.

THE JUBES

In 1955, the Southern Alberta Jubilee Auditorium opened its doors in tandem with the Northern Alberta Jubilee Auditorium in Edmonton, signaling a new era in the culture of the cities.

Over the last 51 years, "the Jube," which seats over 2,500, has hosted a wide range of cultural events, including the Kiwanis Festival, Alberta Ballet and Les Miserables. Stantec Architecture Ltd. oversaw a massive renovation in 2004-05, as part of the province's millennium celebrations.

DANCING WITH JONI

In February 2007, a very special ballet was premiered at the Jube. Legendary songwriter, guitarist, and artist Joni Mitchell who was born Roberta Joan Anderson in Fort Macleod back in 1943, was the inspiration for Alberta Ballet's "Dancing Joni."

Under the eye of creative director and famed choreographer Jean Grand-Maitre, the 48-minute production used nine songs from the iconic Mitchell. Far from being a traditional ballet, the performance drew on the more abstract side of Mitchell's work — her paintings.

Bio A DISTINCT VOICE

There is, perhaps, no more quintessentially Albertan novel than *Who Has Seen the Wind* and there is perhaps no more quintessentially Albertan writer than William Ormond Mitchell. This may sound suspect given Mitchell's Saskatchewan roots, but it was as an Albertan that Mitchell made his mark, conveying in words the landscape and people of Canada's prairie west.

Born in 1914, Mitchell lived in Weyburn, SK until a brush with tuberculosis at the age of 12 took his family to Florida, where the climate restored his health. Mitchell returned to Canada in 1931. After a brief recurrence of his illness, Mitchell vowed to pursue his love of writing. In 1940, he enrolled in the University of Alberta where he earned a BA, a teaching certificate, and met his wife, Merna Hirtle. In 1944, Mitchell and his family settled in High River.

His 1947 *Who has Seen the Wind* was wildly successful, readers seeing in it dark childhood truths and the essence of the prairie west. It was so popular that in 1977 it became a feature film. Numerous novels followed over the next three decades. Though successful in their own rights, none were as enthusiastically greeted as his first. Mitchell also made his mark as a playwrite. His most successful was *Jake and the Kid*. Originally written for Maclean's, it became a weekly CBC radio series from 1950-56 and was televised in 1961. He later parlayed the characters from these stories into *According to Jake and the Kid* (1989) which won the Stephen Leacock award for humour. Other accolades followed. He was a Member of the Order of Canada, an honorary Member of the Privy Council and has several honorary degrees.

In 1968, engagements as writer in residence (including a stint at the University of Calgary) took him from High River, but he later settled in Calgary. It was here that W.O Mitchell died in 1998, having left a mark on all Canadians. As Rex Murphy noted of this massive talent, he will be remembered as "lecturer, performer, stage raconteur, friend of a legion of fledgling writers, . . . a 'presence' in the life and minds of Canadians."

Greatest Outdoor Show On Earth

"The Calgary Stampede will make Buffalo Bill's Wild West extravaganza look like a sideshow," proclaimed Guy Weadick as he promoted what was to become known as the Greatest Outdoor Show on Earth. He was right. What began in 1912 as a small rodeo has evolved into one of the city's — nay, one of the country's — most ingrained institutions. For ten days each July, the entire city embraces the cowboy way. Everyone from bank tellers to CEO's don Stetsons and bolo ties.

Boasting a midway and exhibits of prize livestock, today's Stampede is a sensory smorgasbord that connects Calgary's past and present. The Coca Cola stage hosts some of the biggest names in country and mainstream rock and is packed every night with onlookers climbing the trees to catch a glimpse of who's on stage. Visitors can see all these sights while they enjoy quintessential Stampede fare, including such treats as corn dogs and candy apples.

The whole city celebrates the event with free pancake breakfasts and hay bales on the streets. Corporate fundraisers peddling barbequed Alberta beef and promoting live country entertainment use the Stampede mood to raise hundreds of thousands of dollars for community charities.

The pinnacle moment of the Stampede is its world famous parade, held the first Friday of the event. It brings the city's centre to a standstill as an army of clowns, horses and colourful floats weave their way through the streets. Banks and businesses close their doors for the morning so their employees can attend the popular event.

The Calgary Stampede is a driving political and economic force in the city and Stampede grounds are slated for expansion in 2007 to help meet the demand of the million-plus visitors that stream through the gates every year. The expansion plan has met with some controversy as the residents of the low income Victoria Park have been forced from their homes amid soaring real estate prices.

STAMPEDE BY THE NUMBERS

- Number of people in the first Stampede parade held in 1912 down 8th Avenue (it included 1,500 representatives of the six Tribes of Plains Indians, cowboys, buffalo and bull trains, miners, fur traders and the Royal North West Mounted Police): 3,000

- Number of spectators: 75,000
- Year in which "Wildhorse Jack" Morton began dishing out flapjacks from the back of his chuckwagon, beginning a Calgary Stampede tradition that is as integral a part of the Stampede: 1923
- Number of regular hot dogs consumed during Stampede Week: 125,148
- Number of hamburgers: 76,652
- Number of corn dogs: 96,272
- Number of tons of baked beans: 5 tons
- Number of minutes most of the bucking broncos used at the Stampede (most of the stock live on the Stampede Ranch, located near Hanna) end up working in their entire lifetime: 5
- Year in which Patsy Rogers was crowned the first Miss Calgary Stampede: 1946
- Number of years later two princesses were named to "attend" to the queen, completing what's known as the Royal Trio: 2
- Number of times the British Royal Family has been at the Calgary Stampede: 3
- Year in which the first unofficial chuckwagon race was held, after a couple of cowboys challenged each other after a birthday bash for a local politician: 1919
- Year in which chuckwagon races, simply known as the "chucks" to Calgarians, officially debuted at the Calgary Stampede: 1923
- Number of kilograms of wool that is sheared during the Stampede Super Shear competition: 227
- Year in which Roman races, where one rider races around the track on two horses, was introduced as a possible event at the Stampede: 1919
- Year in which auto polo, promoted as the "climax of the dangerous sports," was attempted to be introduced: 1920
- Year in which ski jumping off the grandstand was introduced: 1921
- Number of horses killed in 1986, after the worst accident in Stampede chuckwagon history: 6
- Length to which the steel used for animal pens at the Stampede would stretch if laid end to end: 34 kms

They Said It

ORCHESTRAL DELIGHT

The Calgary Philharmonic Orchestra (CPO) stages several large-scale concerts throughout the year. The CPO was formed in 1955 when the Calgary Symphony and the Alberta Philharmonic merged. On their 30th anniversary in 1985, they made their permanent home in the EPCOR Centre for the Performing Arts Jack Singer Concert Hall.

One Yellow Rabbit

From its humble beginnings in 1982, the creative collective known as One Yellow Rabbit has grown into one of Calgary's best known theatre troupes.

The trio of Denise Clarke, Michael Greene and Blake Brooker combine dance, spoken word and cutting edge plays and they have become a recognizable group in the performing arts scene. At times controversial, the ensemble has maintained a high profile in Calgary by never bowing to the critics and always following their instincts.

The High Performance Rodeo has become a crowd favourite over the years, marking its 21st anniversary in 2007. Each January, artists from around the world premiere works in theatre, dance, music, poetry and visual arts, providing a quirky, cutting edge festival with a reputation for pushing the envelope. Past participants have included Phillip Glass, Compagnie Marie Chouinard and Calgarian Chris Cran.

During the summer, the group also offers summer school for aspiring actors, writers and directors hoping to start their career in theatre.

Bio LES KIMBER: "THAT'S MY HOLLYWOOD OUT THERE"

Trained in Oregon and Toronto, TV producer Les Kimber cut his teeth in the 1960s at the Calgary's CFCN, before immersing himself in the world of stage acting. He was involved with touring productions of "My Fair Lady" and the "Pajama Game." Eventually he found himself a producer and stage manager for the two companies in town that would later become Theatre Calgary.

His first big film break came when he was hired as manager of Canadian Production for Arthur Penn's "Little Big Man" which was filmed around Calgary. In the 1970s and '80s, he was a prolific producer, working on such movies as Robert Altmans' "Buffalo Bill and the Indians," Michael Ritchie's "Prime Cut" and Arthur Hiller's "Silver Streak."

Between movies, he drove gravel trucks and sold cars. Kimber also traveled to Los Angeles where he lobbied the crème de la crème of Hollywood names and scored some big movies for his hometown. He enticed "Superman One" to film in the Rocky Mountains. He scoured the region for the perfect cave where the superhero lived as a teenager, finding it in the glaciers of the Colombia Icefield.

Later in his career, he worked in television, overseeing such popular series as "Lonesome Dove" and "North of 60." His last project was a Disney movie, "Noah." In 1993, he won the David Billington Award for career achievements and contribution to the film business from Alberta Motion Picture Industries Association.

Kimber, who had a rare reputation for sticking to budgets without sacrificing quality, worked right up until his death in 1998. Kimber insisted he was not in it for the money, but would never comment on how much he made. "Who knows? I haven't counted lately. Let's just say I'm not fading away to nothing."

They Said It

ORDER UP!
- Number of restaurants, bars and caterers in Alberta: 6,878
- Percentage that are independently owned and operated: 55.6
- Number of employees working in the food service industry: 107,500
- Total sales generated from restaurants in Alberta: $5.8 billion
- Share of provincial GDP: 2.9 percent

Source: Alberta; Canadian Restaurant and Foodservices Association.

FAST FOOD
- Number of Tim Horton's in Canada: 2,611
- Number of Tim Horton's in Calgary: 83
- Number of McDonald's in Canada: 1,375
- Number of McDonald's in Calgary: 39
- Number of Piano Bars in Calgary: 4
- Number of Dueling Piano Bars: 2

Did you know...

that Theatre Sports were invented at the Loose Moose Theatre Company in Calgary? Formed in 1977, the improvisational form of sketch performance has taken the comedy world by storm. Co-founder and creative director Dennis Cahill has brought his high-energy brand of entertainment to New York City, Helsinki and Sydney.

Take 5 HOT LITTLE ROCKET'S FIVE SPOTS IN CALGARY TO HANG OUT

Hot Little Rocket have been proud members of Calgary's thriving music community for seven years. In 2005, they traveled to China, performing in front of crowds of thousands and are the only Canadian Indie band to have made the trek to the communist country and have the photos from the Great Wall to prove it.

They just completed recording an album with Steve Albini of Nirvana fame in Chicago and are planning to release the album in 2007.

1: **Tubby Dog:** There is nothing gourmet about it. It's really bad for you; hot dogs that taste great at two in the morning. There's even a hot dog wrapped in bacon, deep fried, and served with a fried egg. They call it the Ultimate Gripper for its heart attack-inducing qualities.

2: **Broken City:** It feels like home. The owners are music fans first. Local bands have the chance to do more avant garde stuff. It's the ultimate place to have a drink and listen to some great music, be it bands or DJ's. The rooftop patio is fantastic in the summer.

3: **The Ship and Anchor Pub:** The richest dive in town. Also home to the best burgers and breakfast on the weekends. Sitting on the patio for people-watching can't be beat. You can be anyone and feel at home here.

4: **Beano:** It's a mecca for artists of all persuasions. It's one of the few truly independent coffee shops that has survived the influx of Starbucks. The benches outside are great for people-watching.

5: **Ming:** It's a martini bar but it's not pretentious. There's tongue in cheek communist propaganda on the walls with food and drinks named after historical political figures. The Red Room has a cool Twin Peaks feel and their ginger beef is the best.

Take 5 FIVE CALGARY SPORTS TEAMS

1. **Calgary Flames** (NHL)
2. **Calgary Hitmen** (WHL)
3. **Calgary Stampeders** (CFL)
4. **Calgary Roughnecks Lacrosse** (NLL)
4. **Calgary Vipers** (NBL)

FESTIVAL FACTS

Calgary is home to a wide variety of music festivals with summer being the peak season. From roots to blues and classical, there is no shortage of talent performing on stages all over the city. Here are some of the more popular music festivals held throughout the year.

- Calgary FolkFest
- CariFest
- Calgary Kiwanis Music Festival
- Honen's International Piano Competition
- C-Jazz
- Afrikadey!
- Expo Latino
- LilacFest
- Beltline Blues Festival
- Calgary International Reggae Festival

Did you know...

that the Caesar cocktail, a concoction of vodka, clamato juice, Worcestershire sauce and Tabasco was invented in the Owl's Nest lobby lounge of Calgary's Westin Hotel?

OOOOO... AHHHHH...

Each August, Calgary is home to a dazzling display of fireworks competitors from around the world, all vying for top prize at GlobalFest. The only event of its kind, organizers bring together pyromusical teams

Bio PRAIRIE PRIDE

Born Paul Rennee Belobersycky in Calgary on July 21st, 1972, Paul Brandt has become one of Alberta's most celebrated singer/songwriters. Although he began his career as a pediatric registered nurse working at the Alberta Children's Hospital in Calgary, he broke onto the country music main stage in 1996 with *Calm Before the Storm*, which spawned four hit singles. He followed up that album with *Outside the Frame* and *A Paul Brandt Christmas (Shall I Play for You)* in 1997 and *That's the Truth* in 1999.

In 2000, Brandt released a greatest hits compilation titled *What I Want to Be Remembered For* and promptly left his record label, successfully starting his own label called Brand-T Records. *Small Towns and Big Dreams* was released in 2001 followed by *This Time Around* in 2004 and *The Gift* in 2006.

To begin his career, Brandt left Alberta for the bright lights of Nashville. He has since moved back home to Calgary, and many of his lyrics emphasize his love for this land, especially the hit "Alberta Bound":

This piece of heaven that I've found
Rocky Mountains and black fertile ground
Everything I need beneath that big blue sky
Doesn't matter where I go
This place will always be my home
Yeah I've been Alberta bound for all my life
And I'll be Alberta bound until I die

from around the world.

Past competitors have been Hong Kong (2006 champion and winner of the people's choice award), Italy and South Africa, who have launched breathtaking combinations of fireworks timed to musical scores. Held at Elliston Park in East Calgary, over 300,000 visitors have stopped to recline on the grass and gasp in wide-eyed wonder since 2003.

As part of this unique and dynamic festival, cultural pavilions in community halls and churches bring all the diversity and richness of the world's different communities to the city. Featuring traditional food, dance, and costumes, it is an engaging and fascinating glimpse into the customs of other countries.

Did you know...

that Tommy Chong, half of the comedy duo Cheech and Chong, was once asked to leave the city of Calgary when his band, the Shades, whipped a crowd into such frenzy that it disgruntled the suburban neighbours? Chong still jokes about being run out of town by the mayor.

Take 5 FIVE CALGARY ACTORS

1. **Paul Gross**
2. **Tommy Chong**
3. **Tom Jackson**
4. **Evangeline Lilly**
5. **Pat Kelly**

HONENS PIANO COMPETITION

Every three years, 21 talented pianists from around the world converge in Calgary for the Honens piano competition. Held in late October, it draws huge crowds and the finals at the Jack Singer Concert Hall consistently sell out, with live nightly broadcasts on CBC Radio2.

Hundreds of thousands of dollars in prizes are awarded to up-and-coming musicians and a unique three-season artistic and career development program is bestowed to the winner.

They Said It

"People tend to forget how important the arts are to culture, to our general everyday lives and the way that art comments on the social norms, ideologies."

– Calgary writer, Sharron Proulx-Turner

They Said It

"Alberta's biggest selling point was that you could live here relatively cheaply and still have a good quality of life. Now that's Saskatchewan. The flight of the creative class is really happening in Calgary right now."

– Sue Bristow, independent film producer

The event is named after Esther Honens, an ardent supporter of the arts in Calgary who donated $5 million to get the competition started. In the years since, it has become an internationally renowned success.

Unfortunately, Honen passed away five days after the competition began in 1992 and was never able to witness her dream.

Take 5 — KIRSTEN KOSLOSKI'S TOP FIVE CALGARY BANDS TO WATCH

Kirsten Kosloski is the music, film and video editor at Fast Forward Weekly, the alternative arts and entertainment magazine in Calgary.

1. **Chad VanGaalen** — Prolific singer-songwriter who got his start as a one-man band playing outside a local pizza joint. Known for being a bit of a recluse, it is rumoured that he has written hundreds of songs in his basement home studio. His latest album Skelliconnection, was released on Sub Pop and local label Flemish Eye. VanGaalen is currently gaining much critical-acclaim in North America and Europe.

2. **The Dudes** — One of the hardest-working rock bands in the country. Their songs are infectious and catchy.

3. **Azeda Booth** — Laptop-electro rock band known for putting on amazing live performances.

4. **The Cape May** — Melodic and dark alt-rock. Their latest album Glass Mountain Roads is a stellar, accomplished release, local or otherwise.

5. **Woodpigeon** — Multi-instrumental pop orchestra with intimate lyrics about love and loss. Their latest album, Songbook, is a soft and touching release.

Weblinks

The Alberta College of Art and Design
www.acad.ab.ca
Now entering its 80th year in Calgary, the Alberta College of Art and Design is a creative online hub with community events, galleries and profiles of the faculty. The Stirring Culture speakers' series in 2005 was wildly successful and a new version is currently under development.

The EPCOR Centre
www.epcorcentre.org
The EPCOR Centre for the performing arts has a bounty of information on theatre, dance, and visual arts. It has everything from event listings to external links to some of Calgary's hottest theatre and performance ensembles.

Tourism Calgary
www.tourismcalgary.com
Compiled by the Calgary Convention and Visitor's Bureau, this site features quick links to a wide range of activities in Calgary and the Rocky Mountains. In addition, the site has an event planner and forms to nominate exemplary Calgarians for a White Hat Award.

Tourism Calgary: The Heart of the New West
www.tourismcalgary.com
With extensive off site links ranging from mid-range to swanky hotels and in depth articles. From the history and importance of the Calgary Stampede to the vibrant arts scene, it's a nicely presented glimpse into Calgary's unique identity.

Economy

Make no mistake about it, Calgary is still very much an oil and gas town. Sure it has learned from past booms and busts, diversifying its base to include transportation, manufacturing and research and development; but still when the price of oil goes up, so, too, do Calgary's fortunes, pulling the whole city along with it.

The city is currently in the midst of its longest and most pronounced boom, and leads the country in GDP. In total, Calgary accounts for almost forty percent of the province's GDP and continues to lead the country in GDP growth.

The city leads the country in a whole host of categories, including the most millionaires per capita, highest self employment rate, most engineers per capita, and so on. It is a "can do" city in a "can do" province and that attitude and optimism has attracted people from around the country.

Sector	GDP %
Finance, Insurance Real Estate and Leasing	20.1
Oil, Gas and Mining	13.5
Transportation and Warehousing	10.7

Manufacturing	10.0
Construction	8.0
Professional, Scientific and Technical Services	6.1
Wholesale Trade	5.4
Retail Trade	5.3
Health Care and Social Assistance	4.1
Education Services	3.5
Public Administration	3.1
Accommodation and Food Services	1.8
Utilities	1.6
Agriculture	0.5
Other	1.8

Source: Calgary Economic Development

ALBERTA TAXES

- Alberta is the only province the country with no provincial sales tax.
- Federal GST : 6 percent
- Personal income tax rates: 10 percent of taxable income
- Small business corporate tax rate: 3 percent

Canada Customs and Revenue Agency

TAX FREEDOM DAY

Tax freedom day (date on which earnings no longer go to taxes, 2007)

Nationally	June 19
Alberta	June 1
New Brunswick	June 14
Prince Edward Island	June 14
Manitoba	June 16
British Columbia	June 16
Ontario	June 19
Nova Scotia	June 19
Saskatchewan	June 14
Quebec	July 26

Newfoundland and Labrador   July 1

Source: The Fraser Institute.

COST OF LIVING

Survey compares cost of living at all salary levels. The table shows the family income required in each city to maintain the standard of living associated with three income scenarios.

INCOME LEVELS

CITY	$60,000	$80,000	$100,000
Edmonton	$61,830	$81,142	$99,902
Calgary	$62,818	$82,109	$105,317
Ottawa	$63,168	$84,102	$104,699
Phoenix	$66,523	$88,306	$107,644
Montreal	$68,167	$92,594	$113,884
Vancouver	$69,009	$90,927	$112,647
Minneapolis	$70,961	$93,624	$113,927
Toronto	$74,114	$96,439	$122,627
Seattle	$73,723	$98,441	$118,048
Boston	$84,896	$112,115	$133,384
San Jose	$101,077	$144,029	$164,435

Sources: MMK Consulting and Runzheimer Canada

WHERE THE MONEY GOES

Calgary households spend an average $85,553 a year. Here's how it broke down:

- Income tax: $20,344 (23.8 percent)
- Shelter: $15,270 (17.8 percent)
- Transportation: $10,090 (12.8 percent)
- Food: $8,097 (9.5 percent)
- Insurance/pension payments: $4,516 (5.3 percent)
- Household operation: $3,763 (4.4 percent)
- Clothing: $3,471 (4.1 percent)
- Monetary gifts/contributions: $2,347 (2.7 percent)

- Health care: $2,260 (2.6 percent)
- Tobacco and alcohol: $1,887 (2.2 percent)
- Education: $1,746 (2.0 percent)
- Personal care: $1,393 (1.6 percent)
- Reading material: $338 (0.4 percent)
- Games of chance: $283 (0.3 percent)

Source: Statistics Canada.

On average, Albertans owed $58,400. Amount owing on:
- Mortgages: $78,100
- Lines of credit: $14,500
- Vehicle loans: $13,000
- Student loans: $ 9,200
- Credit cards/installments: $3,400
- Other: $11,700

Source: Statistics Canada.

INCOME
Since 2000, the median income for Calgarians rose from $60,800 to $75,400.

MINIMUM WAGE
- At $7/hr, Alberta's minimum wage ties for last place with New Brunswick and Newfoundland and Labrador.
- Alberta's average hourly wage is the highest in the country at $21.60

GROWING PAINS
- Percentage of Calgarians who say they believe the current pace of growth for the province of Alberta is not manageable, according to a survey by Leger Marketing: 50
- Percentage of Edmontonians who say they believe the current pace of growth for the province of Alberta is not manageable: 41

TODD HIRSCH'S TOP FIVE
REASONS WHY CALGARY'S ECONOMY
IS THE BEST IN THE COUNTRY

Todd Hirsch holds a BA in Economics from the University of Alberta and an MA in Economics from the University of Calgary. He is currently the Chief Economist for the Canada West Foundation, and teaches economics at the University of Calgary. He is a regular contributor to *Calgary Inc. Magazine, Avenue Magazine, Policy Options* and the *Globe and Mail.*

1. **Oil and Gas:** Calgary is the uncontested energy capital of the country. The "oil patch" employs thousands of highly paid professionals, and many business and personal services benefit indirectly.

2. **Entrepreneurial Spirit:** Calgary has the youngest and most highly educated workforce of any major city in Canada. There is a strong ethos that with a good idea and hard work you can really get ahead here.

3. **A City of Volunteers:** Going back two decades, Calgary gained a reputation for volunteerism during the 1988 Winter Olympic Games — still one of the most financially successful Olympics ever. Calgarians can always be counted on to roll up their sleeves for a good cause.

4. **The Rocky Mountains:** The city rests in the shadows of one of the most beautiful natural areas in the world — a major international tourist draw!

5. **The Heart of the New West:** As economic and political clout in Canada shifts even more to western Canada, Calgary is increasingly the undisputed business, financial and political heart of the region.

Take 5 — TOP FIVE LARGEST ENERGY SECTOR EMPLOYERS IN CALGARY
(NUMBER OF EMPLOYEES)

1. **Precision Drilling Corporation** (12,000)
2. **ATCO Ltd.** (7,531)
3. **Ensign Resource Service Group Inc.** (7,300)
4. **Flint Energy Services Ltd.** (4,600)
5. **Petro Canada** (4,500)

Source: Calgary Economic Development.

HOW WE GET TO WORK

- 78 percent use automobiles
- 15.4 percent use public transit
- 6.6 percent walk or cycle

Source: University of Calgary.

THE CALGARY COMMUTE

- The average Canadian spends nearly 12 full days each year traveling between home and work, which works out to approximately 63 minutes a day.
- The Toronto commute, the longest in Canada: 79 minutes a day
- Calgary has among the fastest growing commute times. In 2005, Calgarians spent 66 minutes a day commuting, a full 14 minutes more each day over the average commute in 1992.

Source: Statistics Canada.

Did you know...

that the Conference Board of Canada has predicted the price of oil will remain above US$65 barrel for the next five years?

King of Beers

You don't normally think that having too many whiskeys might lead to the establishment of one of the most successful brewery launches in recent Canadian history, but that is precisely what happened to Ed McNally. McNally and his friend Otto Leverkus were having drinks one evening when Leverkus mentioned he loved Alberta but missed the beers of his native Germany. The two joked that McNally should start a brewery to remedy the situation. Six months later Leverkus telephoned McNally to tell him he had found a brewmaster.

That, of course, is only part of the McNally's story. His first career was that of a Calgary lawyer who came to successfully represent a group of Alberta barley farmers in a case against the Canadian Wheat Board. In short order, he became a member of the Board of Directors of the Alberta Barley Growers. He quickly recognized that Alberta's barley was some of the best in the world for brewing. Lawyer McNally became barley farmer McNally. It was only a matter of time that farmer McNally became brewery owner McNally.

He hired brewmaster Bernd Pieper in 1984 and Calgary's Big Rock Brewery was born. Sales ballooned for McNally's high quality unpasteurized beer, helped by sales of the wildly popularly Pale Ale, which was introduced in 1986 just as strikes crippled larger Alberta breweries. Big Rock made great strides showcasing its wares during the 1988 Olympic games and is now the 15th largest brewery in North America. Other beers with colourful names like Grasshopper, Jack Rabbit and Warthog have been developed and are now Alberta staples.

McNally is a Calgary icon and as colourful as some of the names of his beers. He is an avid fly fisherman and you can find him on rivers and streams anywhere in the province. He was one of the first business people to come to ranchers' aid during the BSE scare. He is member of the Order of Canada and was granted an honourary doctorate of laws from the University of Lethbridge.

You Said How Much

Wage data is hourly and is taken from the latest available data.

Jarome Iginla, right wing for the Calgary Flames	$3589.74
Calgary Mayor Bronconnier	$64.62
Dentists	$50.05
Veterinarians	$45.57
Senior government managers and officials	$44.88
Lawyers	$41.95
Financial managers	$41.11
Civil engineers	$40.69
Constable first class, Calgary police	$38.45
Pharmacists	$38.24
School principals	$35.67
Carpenters	$35.20
Software engineers	$34.99
Physiotherapists	$30.87
Occupational therapists	$30.84
Pipe fitters	$29.80
Secondary school teachers	$27.14
Registered nurses	$27.04
Plumbers	$25.04
Social workers	$24.99
Elementary school teachers	$24.85
Welders	$24.78
Electricians	$24.21
Retail managers	$23.29
Graphic designers	$22.20
Oil and gas well diggers and workers	$21.57
Heavy equipment mechanics	$21.55
Auto mechanics	$20.20
Legal secretaries	$19.59
Heavy equipment operators	$19.28
Editors	$17.17
Medical secretaries	$14.61
Janitors	$13.18

Source: Human Resource Development Canada; NHL; City of Calgary.

Take 5 **TOP FIVE LARGEST ENERGY COMPANIES IN CALGARY (REVENUE)**

1. **Imperial Oil** ($22.4 billion)
2. **EnCana Corp** ($15.4 billion)
3. **Petro Canada** ($14.7 billion)
4. **Shell Canada Ltd.** ($11.2 billion)
5. **Husky Energy Ltd.** ($8.4 billion)

Source: Calgary Economic Development.

NO PARKING

- Median cost of a monthly parking (unreserved rate) in Calgary as of mid-2006: $375
- Median cost in Edmonton; $140
- Median cost in Toronto: $300
- Median cost in Montreal: $259
- Median cost in Vancouver: $194
- Canadian average: $194.51
- Rank of Calgary among cities with the most expensive monthly or daily parking rates: 1

Source: Colliers International.

POVERTY AMIDST PLENTY

Not all Calgarians are reaping rewards of the booming economy. In 2006, 17 percent of employed Calgarians age 15 or older earned less than $12 an hour. More than 60 percent of them were women.

Source: Vibrant Communities Calgary

Did you know...

that of the city of Calgary's tax-supported budget, property taxes make up $6.32 million or 20 percent?

O . . . T
- Percentage of Montrealers who work more than 50 hours a week: 7
- Percentage of Vancouverites: 16
- Percentage of Torontonians: 20
- Percentage of Calgarians: 24
- Percentage of Edmontonians: 28

Source: Bank of Montreal.

Bio CLIVE BEDDOE: A HIGH FLIER

As a real estate developer with the Hanover Group of Companies, Clive Beddoe found himself traveling a lot for business and grew frustrated with the high cost of flying with standard commercial airlines. A licensed pilot, Beddoe decided to set up a no nonsense airline with tickets being replaced by confirmation numbers and light snacks instead of full meals.

Although the wages were slightly lower than their counterparts, WestJet attracted vibrant young employees, earning the airline a fresh and breezy reputation. It was an immediate success. Within months of starting, flights were added to Victoria, Regina and Saskatoon. By 1999, two years after they began flying, Thunder Bay, Prince George and Grande Prairie were added to a growing list of destinations. WestJet now has flights throughout Canada and the U.S and competes with Air Canada for passengers.

Beddoe's career has not been without some turbulence. In 2004, he was accused of spying on Air Canada and after reaching a deal with his biggest competitor, he made a public apology and donated $10 million to charity.

He announced in September 2006 that within the next year, he was stepping down as CEO of the popular airline at the age of 60.

They Said It

"Alberta is in the midst of the strongest period of economic growth ever recorded by any Canadian province."

– Statistics Canada

BUSINESSES IN CALGARY

Calgary's entrepreneurial reputation is well-deserved. In all, in 2006, there were approximately 51,910 businesses. By far, the vast majority – 93.5 percent – were small businesses with fewer than 50 employees. In fact, 55 percent of all businesses had fewer than four employees.

- Total number of small businesses: 48,536
- Number with 1-4 employees: 28,841 (59.4 percent)
- 5-9 employees: 8,546 (17.6 percent)
- 10-19 employees: 6,323 (13 percent)
- 20-49 employees: 4,826 (10 percent)

Calgary is home to the highest number of small business per capita in Canada, at 40.3 per 1,000 people. Here's how other major centres compare (number per 1,000 people).

- Vancouver: 38.4
- Edmonton: 36.4
- Toronto: 28.2
- Ottawa: 27.1
- Montreal: 24.5

Did you know...

that 40 percent of inbound shipments received at the port of Vancouver are sent to Calgary?

SMALL BUSINESS GROWTH

Calgary recorded Canada's greatest growth in small business between 2002 and 2006, when small businesses in the city grew by 7.9 percent. Here's how other cities measured up over this same period.

Vancouver: 7.4 percent
Edmonton: 6.4 percent
Toronto: 5.5 percent
Ottawa: 1.7 percent
Montreal: -0.7 percent

SELF-EMPLOYMENT

Calgary is also tops when it comes to self-employment. In all, 105,200 Calgarians work for themselves, or 95 per 1,000 people. How do other cities compare? (Number per 1,000)
Vancouver: 93.7
Toronto: 76.9
Edmonton: 75.1
Ottawa: 69.3
Montreal: 67.1

Self-employment is a growing trend in Calgary. Between 2002 -2006, the number of self-employed Calgarians ballooned by 22.8 percent, the great-

Take 5 FIVE LARGEST TRANSPORTATION AND LOGISTICS COMPANIES (REVENUE)

1. **Canadian Pacific Railway** ($3.9 billion)
2. **West Jet** ($1.1 billion)
3. **Trimac Holdings Ltd.** ($638 million)
4. **Greyhound Canada Transport Corporation** ($329.4 million)
5. **The Calgary Airport Authority** ($126.6 million)

est increase in Canada. Consider the growth rates in the following cities:

Edmonton: 22.1 percent

Montreal: 13.9 percent

Vancouver: 12.7 percent

Toronto: 9.9 percent

Ottawa: 2 percent

YOUTH ON OUR SIDE

Calgary's entrepreneurial cohort has a strong future in large measure because of its youth. Compared to other major cities, it has the largest proportion of self-employed people who are ages 15-35: 20.1 percent.

Edmonton: 19.3 percent

Ottawa: 19.2 percent

Montreal: 18.4 percent

Toronto: 17.6 percent

Vancouver: 16.3 percent

BANKRUPTCIES

In 2006, 267 Calgary businesses went bankrupt. The good news is that the rate of bankruptcies is down by 52 percent since 1997, a year that recorded 558 bankruptcies.

Source: Calgary Economic Development,

Take 5 — TOP FIVE LARGEST EMPLOYERS
(TOTAL NUMBER OF EMPLOYEES)

1. **Canada Safeway** (30,000)
2. **Westfair Foods** (29,000)
3. **Calgary Health Region** (18,000)
4. **Canadian Pacific Railway Co.** (16,106)
5. **The Forzani Group** (10,733)

Source: Alberta Economic Update.

CALGARY HAS THE . . .

- Highest employment growth in 2006 at 7.7%
- Highest total employment growth at a rate of 38.8% over the past 10 years (1997-2006)
- Highest average annual employment growth at 3.8% over the past 10 years (1997-2006)

HOUSING

- Value of building permits issued in 2006 for residential & commercial projects: $4.76 billion
- Value by which this exceeds the city of Toronto: $1 billion
- Number of new homes being built per day during 2006: 45
- Number of development and building department staff hired by the city of Calgary as a result of the housing boom: 60

Source: City of Calgary

Did you know...

that overall housing prices increased by 40 percent in 2006?

Take 5 TOP FIVE MOST EXPENSIVE
PROPOSED PROJECTS (PROJECTED COST)

1. **EnCana's Bow Office Tower** ($850,000,000)
2. **Calgary Airport Authority Airport Improvements** ($850,000,000)
3. **Tsuu T'ina Nation Business Centre** ($670,000,000)
4. **Alberta Cancer Board - Replacement Building for Tom Baker Cancer Centre**($600,000,000)
5. **Calgary Health Region Hospital for South Calgary** ($550,000,000)

Source: AlbertaFirst.

HIGHER AND HIGHER

In January, 2007 the City of Calgary mailed approximately 400,000 property assessment notices.

- The median single residential assessment value (excluding condos) is $361,000.
- The median improved condo assessment is $225,000.
- The typical market value residential increase over the previous year is 43 percent.
- The typical market value non-residential increase is 42.8 percent.

UP AND UP

In Calgary, 206 homes have sold for more than $1 million in 2006, up 124 per cent. The most expensive home sold in 2006 was $3.4 million.

Did you know...

that in 2005, Calgary's labour force was the most robust in Canada at $76,961 real GDP?

COST OF A HOUSE
Calgary, selected regions

	North	North Inner City	South Inner City	West
Detached Bungalow	$330,400	$446,200	$433,800	$385,000
Standard 2 Storey	$365,400	$489,700	$506,400	$402,600
Standard Condo	$229,900	$266,800	$278,900	$252,400
Standard Townhouse	$277,000	$339,800	$323,300	$305,000

Source: Royal LePage.

WHAT CALGARIANS SPEND
The average household expenses are 20 percent higher than in Saskatoon, with Calgarians spending $8,097 on food annually and $10,090 on travel.

Source: Statistics Canada.

INFRASTRUCTURE
Calgary International Airport (CIA), Canada's fourth busiest, is highly regarded. In 2004, J.D. Power and Associates ranked CIA number one in passenger satisfaction in its Global Airport Satisfaction Index Study. In addition, the CIA is the only Canadian airport with 24/7 cargo services to Asia and Europe.

- Number of global cities served by flights out of the CIA: 66
- Total number of passengers served annually: 11.3 million
- Numbers who are domestic travelers: 8.1
- Numbers who are traveling trans-border: 2.2 million
- Number traveling internationally: 900,000

No Business Like . . .

If there is a single difference between Canadian and American entrepreneurs, it is the quiet factor. A U.S. tycoon is much heralded figure. In Canada and in Calgary, you are just as likely to unknowingly pass them in the Safeway. One of Canada richest and most famous families is Calgary's Mannix clan, who may take the prize for the most silent of the quiet.

The Mannix family fortune had its beginnings in the construction trade when a young Manitoba farm boy named Fred Mannix picked up and moved to Calgary. The third generation of Mannix family members (Fred III and Ron) now run the family group of companies, estimated to be worth more than $2 billion.

They preside over a company that continues to be involved in the construction trade as well as the coal and oil and gas industry, including pipelines, venture capital and railroad maintenance services. They were at one time was involved in the building of subways in Montreal and Toronto, the St. Lawrence Seaway, the Trans-Canada Highway, the Grand Coulee Dam and the Cold-War-era Dew Line.

In typical fashion, the family has quietly played an active philanthropy role. In 1998, the family gave away $100 million through the Carthy Foundation, at the time the single largest cash donation in Canadian history. The family has also been instrumental in the founding of the University of Alberta's Alberta Business Family Institute at the University.

As Ron Mannix recently put it, there's no business like a family business. There is better management, he said, and in most cases,there are better products. There's a willingness to invest in research and innovative technology with long-term planning. There are many, many advantages family business has over public enterprises.

RAIL

Calgary businesses have ready access to rail transport. The city is a major stop on both the Canadian Pacific (CP) and Canadian National (CN) railways. In 1996, CN moved its headquarters to Calgary, and each year 50,000 rail cars from across the continent pass through its new intermodal facility based in the city. Calgary is also home to CN's third largest Canadian intermodal terminal.

Source: Calgary Economic Development

DOWNTOWN OFFICE SPACE (MILLIONS OF SQUARE FEET)

Toronto	59.4
Montreal	50.0
Calgary	**32.1**
Vancouver	22.6
Edmonton	14.0
Ottawa	14.0
Winnipeg	12.9
Victoria	7.8

MORE SPACE

- Estimated number of new jobs in Calgary between 2006 and 2010 that will require additional office space, according to a study conducted by urbanMetrics Inc.: 25,000
- Estimated total amount of office space required to accommodate this short-term growth: 49 million
- Estimated total amount of office space Calgary will reach by 2010 based on current development: 57.5 million

Did you know...

that of all Canadian cities, only Toronto has more corporate headquarters than Calgary?
Source: Government of Canada

FLIGHT TIMES TO/FROM CALGARY

Ottawa 3 h 50 m
Toronto 4 h 10 m
Vancouver 1 h 15 m
Dallas 3 h 40 m
Los Angeles 3 h
New York City 5 h 3 m
London, UK 8 h, 45 m
Frankfurt 9 h 20 m
Tokyo 10 h 25 m

CALGARY DOWNTOWN

In all, 12,000 Calgarians work in the city's downtown and 32,000 call it home – and both numbers are on the rise. In 2006, 12 residential towers and five commercial building projects were underway. All is not concrete and steel in the downtown, however. Across the city, including in the downtown, 10 percent of land is reserved for green spaces and school construction.

DOWNTOWN CALGARY

- Number of stores: 1000+
- Number of shopping centers/department stores: 11
- Number of dining spots: 200+
- Number of nightclubs: 50+
- Number of movie screens: 10
- Number of historic spots: 50+
- Number of theatres: 13
- Number of tourist attractions: 18

Did you know...

that the only North American city that has more employees in oil and gas than Calgary (32,400) is Houston, TX (66,700)?

- Number major festivals each year: 25
- Number public spaces/parks: 13
- Number of parking spots: 47,000
- Number of free Sunday parking spots: 3000
- Number of businesses downtown: 3,500
- Number of head offices: 76
- Number of commercial office buildings: 124

Source: Downtown Calgary Association.

GAS AND OIL

The energy sector, the heartbeat of Calgary's economy and the root of its prosperity, generates 13 percent of the city's GDP. Of the $108 billion worth of energy-related projects in all of Alberta, a whopping $75 billion worth are centred in Calgary. Calgary is home to the vast majority of Canada's oil and gas production companies, major pipeline operators, oilfield service and drilling companies and energy-related engineering and consulting firms. It also headquarters major North American pipeline and energy distribution companies.

Every tick upward in the price of oil further stokes an already heated Calgary and Alberta economy. Provincial revenues increase by $65 million for every dollar increase in the price of oil, and oil royalty revenue now accounts for almost thirty percent of the provincial budget.

The impact of the gas and oil industry is felt in every aspect of life in the city. It has fuelled the current construction boom and given the city a sense optimism that is unparalled anywhere else in the country.

Did you know...

that Calgary is home to the largest number of head offices per capita in Canada?

They Said It

"How many men do you know who let their religion interfere with their business?"

– Bob Edwards, the Eye Opener, December 6, 1913

OIL SANDS
- Size of the proven oil reserves, in barrels, of Saudia Arabia: 262 billion
- Size of the oil in the underground deposits known collectively as the tarsands around the area of Fort McMurray, the largest lode of hydrocarbons in the world: 1.6 trillion
- Number of barrels considered recoverable with current technology: 174 billion
- Number of barrels considered recoverable with emerging, but not yet established technology: 311 billion
- Number of barrels a day Alberta produces today: 1.594 million
- Number of those that are from the oil sands: 964,000
- Number from conventional sources: 630,000
- Cost to recover is $7 versus 12

Source: Alberta Ministry of Energy.

CANADA CALLING
- Percentage of Canada's oil production accounted for by Alberta, according to the Canadian Association of Petroleum Producers: 72
- Percentage of Canada's natural gas production accounted for by Alberta: 78

Did you know...

that every dollar spent at the Calgary Stampede generates $2.80 for the city of Calgary?

CAPITAL CASE
- Total capital expenditures in Alberta's oil and gas sector as of 2006: $32.9 billion
- Total capital expenditures in Alberta's non-energy sector as of 2006: $18 billion

CALGARIANS EMPLOYED IN THE ENERGY SECTOR
- Total: 32,400
- Oil and Gas Exploration and Production: 20,198
- Oil and Gas Services and Supply: 7,522
- Electric Power Generation, Transmission and Distribution: 2,412
- Pipeline Operation: 1,763
- Petroleum and Coal Products Manufacturing: 248
- Oil Sands and Heavy Oil Development: 172
- Coal Production: 85

CALGARY COMPANIES INVOLVED IN THE ENERGY SECTOR
- Total: 1,854
- Oil and Gas Exploration and Production: 1,059
- Oil and Gas Services and Supply: 682
- Pipeline Operation: 55
- Electric Power Generation, Transmission and Distribution: 34
- Petroleum and Coal Products Manufacturing: 13
- Oil Sands and Heavy Oil Development: 9
- Coal Production: 2

Did you know...

that beef is Alberta's number one agri-food cash cow for export, bringing in $1.4 billion each year?

CASH REGISTER

- Total revenue from non-renewable resources to the Alberta government in fiscal year 2000-01: $10.586 billion
- Actual amount in 2005-2006, double what it was two years ago, and five times what it was in the 1990s: $14.6 billion

WHAT TO DO

- Responding to the question of what the government should do with unexpected oil revenues of $7 billion, percentage of Albertans who said spend the money on improving existing government programs and services, according to a survey done for the Canada West Foundation: 37
- Percentage who said divide up the money and give it to individual Albertans: 14

MOVERS AND SHAKERS

Calgary is fast becoming a hub of transportation industry in Canada. Home to the fourth busiest airport in Canada, Calgary is also strategically centred on the North American highway grid. The city sits at the intersection of the east-west Trans-Canada Highway. It is also conveniently located on the north-south CANAMEX Highway which, when completed, will link Mexico City to Edmonton via a four-lane thoroughfare.

Not surprisingly, transportation and warehousing accounts for a tenth of the city's GDP and employs 46,000 Calgarians who work for 4,189 companies.

Source: Calgary Economic Development; Government of Canada

CALGARIANS EMPLOYED BY THE TRANSPORTATION AND WAREHOUSING SECTOR (2004)

- Total: 46,200
- Wholesaling, Warehouse Distribution and Storage: 19,500
- Truck Transportation: 8,300
- Air Transportation: 6,500
- Postal and Courier Service: 4,600
- Transit and Sightseeing Transportation: 4,200
- Rail Transportation: 3,100

A BILLION DOLLAR INDUSTRY

- Tourism is a billion dollar industry in Calgary.
- More than four million people visit the city annually, spending close to a billion dollars. The industry employs almost 19,000 people.

Source: Tourism Calgary.

Did you know...

that Alberta's total goods export increased by 197.4 percent between 1995 and 2005? Canada's total goods export increased only 65.4 percent in the same time frame.

Weblinks

Calgary Economic Development

www.calgaryeconomicdevelopment.com/index.cfm

With the slogan 'Heart of the New West,' the Calgary Economic Development website has a bounty of lively facts about the city in addition to helpful links to other sites including employment, tourism and government agencies.

Calgary Chamber of Commerce

www.calgarychamber.com

To find out about all things business in Calgary, check out this website maintained by the Calgary Chamber of Commerce.

Association of Professional Engineers, Geologists and Geophysicists of Alberta

www.apegga.org

Featuring resources and detailed information for engineering graduates from around the world, this site is comprehensive and informative for those in the business of building, or for anyone curious about engineering.

Politics

Calgary has been an important national player in the development of new and innovative policy. Largely misunderstood in the rest of the country (the perception being that of a far-right leaning policy), Calgary and Calgarians have historically shown a willingness to embrace a practical approach to problem solving.

The Co-operative Commonwealth Foundation (CCF) in 1932 and the Social Credit Party in 1935, were early examples of Calgarians willingness to experiment. Present-day federal Conservatives can trace their lineage to deep Calgarian roots. While the city is proudly right-of-centre, it has taken on the challenges posed by its population explosion with the same practical 'can-do' attitude that defies political categorization.

TOTAL OPERATING BUDGETS APPROVED BY CALGARY CITY COUNCIL

- 2005: $1.8 billion
- 2006: $1.9 billion
- 2007: $2.0 billion
- 2008: $2.1 billion

Source: City of Calgary.

HIGH COST OF GOVERNMENT (2006)

In 2006 it cost the city $1.62 billion to operate. The biggest single expense was policing, which was $240.5 million, or nearly 15 percent, of the total budget. Here's where the rest was spent:

- General government: $183.8 million (11.3 percent)
- Roads, traffic, parking: 141.9 million (8.7 percent)
- Fire services: $125.3 million (7.7 percent)
- Parks and recreation: $120.6 million (7.4 percent)
- Public works: $94.2 million (5.8 percent)
- Interest and financing fees: $88.8 million (5.5 percent)
- Water waste treatment and disposal: $68.3 million (4.2 percent)
- Water supply and distribution: $56.8 million (3.5 percent)
- Waste and recycling: $53.0 million (3.3 percent)
- Emergency medical services: $49.2 million (3.0 percent)
- Community and social development: $46.1 million (2.8 percent)
- Calgary Public Library: $35.7 million (2.2 percent)
- Societies and related authorities: $21.8 million (1.3 percent)
- Real estate services: $20.6 million (1.3 percent)

Source: City of Calgary,

WHERE CALGARY GETS ITS CASH (PERCENT)

- Sales of goods and services: 29
- Residential property tax: 19
- Non-residential property tax: 19
- Franchise fees, utilities revenue tax, municipal surcharge: 9
- Business tax: 8
- Investment income, reserves and other: 7

Did you know...

that Calgary conducted its first Civic Census in 1931?

- Licenses and permits: 5
- Grants/subsidies: 3
- Fiscal stability reserves: 1

Source: City of Calgary

Bio GEORGE MURDOCH:

The first mayor of Calgary was a young Scot named George Murdoch. Born in 1850, Murdoch was a worldly 33 years old when he made his way to Calgary. At the time, the settlement consisted of a few ramshackle tents along the riverbanks.

With the coming of the railway, however, the community grew and Murdoch led the charge for incorporation, and in so doing became the first mayor. One of the elements of the Northwest Territories Act included a law that forbade the purchase of alcohol. Many in the territory, particularly those in Calgary, flouted the law on a regular basis and were often treated leniently by men like Murdoch.

Murdoch did come to have an adversary in the name of Jeremiah Travis, a happily abstaining magistrate appointed by Ottawa. Travis had jailed a local saloon owner – who was also a town councilor – opening the door for Murdoch and his own soapbox. Murdoch defended the sale and consumption of liquor, first at home and then in Ottawa, earning the adoration of his local townsmen who re-elected him with an overwhelming majority in 1886. In short order Travis had him – and his council – removed from office, and fined Murdoch $200.

Travis put Murdoch's personal belongings on the auction block to cover the fine, but because of his popularity no one would bid on them. Travis was suspended shortly thereafter and the law eventually repealed. Murdoch was never again mayor though he did continue to serve on council and contribute to city life.

Take 5 — CALGARY'S TOP FIVE
LONGEST SERVING MAYORS

1. **Andrew Davison** – 16 years
2. **Alfred Duerr** – 12 years
3. **Donald Mackay** – 8 years, 10 months
4. **Ralph Klein** – 8 years, 5 months
5. **James Sykes** – 8 years

Source: City of Calgary

CITY DEBT

Calgary is in debt to the tune of $1.77 billion, up from $1.54 billion in 2005.

PROPERTY TAXES

Based on a sample house as defined as a 25 to 30 year-old detached 3-bedroom bungalow with a main floor area of 1,200 square feet, finished full basement and a double car garage, on a 6,000 square foot lot. Utility charges include telephones, power, water, sewer, land drainage and garbage collection.

Ottawa	$4,659
Toronto	$4,624
Saskatoon	$4,487
Vancouver	$4,216
Regina	$4,184
St. John's	$4,082
Edmonton	$3889
Calgary	$3708
Fredericton	$3, 694
Montreal	$3,644
Winnipeg	$3,577
Halifax	$3,402

Bio "BIBLE BILL"

One of Canada's most colourful politicians, William "Bible Bill" Aberhart wove his innovative political ideology into the fabric of Calgary's political tapestry. Born in 1878 in Kippen, Ontario, Aberhart was deeply religious and a career in teaching narrowly won out over a ministry in the Baptist church.

In 1910, Aberhart, his wife and two daughters moved to Calgary. There he was a school principal and, before long, an unofficial minister in a local Baptist church and in his own Calgary Prophetic Bible Institute. Calgarians were receptive to Aberhart's fiery sermons and innovative political views.

In 1925, his sermons were so popular that he became host of a wildly successful weekly radio broadcast called Back to the Bible. Each week, 30,000 people across Canada and the United States tuned in. In the 1930's, with Calgary in the grips of the Great Depression, Aberhart sought a solution to wide scale unemployment and he found it in the economic theories of C.H. Douglas.

Douglas' "social credit" theory posited that capitalism's inherent flaw was that it inevitably caused citizens' decreased purchasing power. The key to overcoming this problem, Douglas believed, was to tightly regulate credit and to provide consumers state-sponsored discounts. Aberhart, smitten with this "social credit" philosophy, fused it with his own brand of Christianity and peddled it as a political platform.

When the ruling United Farmers of Alberta party shunned Aberhart's ideas, he organized his own Social Credit Party. Promising citizens a "basic dividend" of $25 monthly, in August 1935, Aberhart and his Social Credit Party won an astounding 56 of 63 seats in the Alberta legislature.

While Social Credit monetary policies ended in failure, Aberhart's penchant for silencing an often-critical press disconcerted Albertans. He managed reelection in 1940, but by then the Social Credit Party's more radical ideas had been excised and the party was more traditionally conservative.

Calgary Mayors

Mayor	Term Served	Profession
George Murdoch	1884-1886	saddlemaker
George Clift King	1886-1888	postmaster
Arthur Edwin Shelton	1888-1889	carpenter
Daniel Webster March	1889-1890	physician
James Delamere Lafferty	1890-1891	physician
James Reilly	1891-1892	architect
Alexandar Lucas	1892-1894	insurance/auctioneer
Wesley Fletcher Orr	1894-1896	journalist/editor
Alexander McBride	1896-1897	business owner
Arthur Leslie Cameron	1898-1899	lumber business
William Henry Cushing	1900-1901	lumber business
James Stuart Mackie	1901-1902	stationary business
Thomas Underwood	1902-1904	contractor
Silas Alexander Ramsey	1904-1905	machinery business
John Emerson	1905-1907	grocery business
Reuben Rupert Jamieson	1907-1911	CPR superintendent
John William Mitchell	1911-1913	lumber business
Herbert Arthur Sinnott	1913-1915	educator
Michael Copps Costello	1915-1919	physician

Mayor	Term Served	Profession
Robert Colin Marshall	1919-1921	contractor
Samuel Hunter Adams	1921-1923	educator
George Harry Webster	1923-1926	railway construction
Frederick Ernest Osborne	1927-1929	bookseller
Andrew Davidson	1930-1945	publisher
James Cameron Watson	1946-1947	electrician
Donald Hugh Mackay	1950-1951	broadcasting
Harry William Hays	1959-1963	exporter
Grant Macewan	1963-1965	agriculture/ animal husbandry
John Clifford Leslie	1965-1965	real estate
James Rodney Winter Sykes	1969-1977	accountant
Ross Patterson Alger	1977-1980	business administration
Ralph Phillip Klein	1980-1989	journalist
Donald Adam Hartman	1989-1989	energy business
Alfred Herman Duerr	1989-2001	urban development
David Thomas Bronconnier	2001-present	insurance contractor

Source: City of Calgary.

Did you know...

CITY GOVERNMENT

The current wardship system, featuring one councilor for each of the city's 14 wards, was put in place in 1976. Meeting monthly and operating on a council-policy committee system, the city council makes all its major decisions based on the findings from four standing committees: operations and environment, finance, transportation and community services.

White Hat

Traditionally, a white cowboy hat was something of an oddity. After all, such a topper is hardly practical in the dusty and dirty cowboy world. After WW II, however, there was greater demand for light-coloured hats and Calgary's own Smithbilt Hats began to make a white version using expensive Russian felt. The first of their stylish white hats debuted and proved wildly successful at the 1947 Stampede Parade.

In 1948, when the Calgary Stampeders won a place in the CFL championship against Ottawa, a delegation of 250 Stampeder fans traveled to the Toronto game, bedecked in the same white hats that would bob along the streets of the city when the Stampeders won it all. As a token of thanks for hosting the game, Toronto's mayor was presented with one of the coveted hats.

One of the merry Calgary football fans that year was a young alderman named Don McKay. By 1950, McKay was Calgary's mayor and it was under his watch that the city began to distribute white hats to visiting dignitaries and a tradition was born. In 1958, Tourism Calgary took over the job of bestowing the now famous symbols, and to this day, hundreds are presented to honour visitors each year.

MAYOR DAVE BRONCONNIER'S
TOP FIVE REASONS
I LOVE BEING MAYOR OF CALGARY

Dave Bronconnier is Calgary's 35th mayor. He was first elected in 2001, following nine years as alderman for Ward 6. Prior to running for elected office, Mayor Bronconnier was a successful business-man in the construction industry. Mayor Bronconnier is one of Canada's most outspoken mayors, and has moved forward an impressive agenda of infrastructure construction, sustainable plan-ning and urban development, environmental stewardship, as well as taking a leadership role in re-balancing the fiscal relationship between municipalities and other orders of government.

Friendly People – Calgarians are known throughout the world for their hospitality. Calgary doesn't have a key to the city, we have a white Smithbilt hat, and when visitors receive one, they know they are among friends.

Volunteer Spirit – Calgary is the Volunteer Capital of Canada. More Calgarians donate their time and their dollars to making this community a better place to live than any other city in the country. That's something we're all very proud of.

Calgary is a city built by entrepreneurs – The entrepreneurial spirit is alive and well in Calgary. Our frontier days are behind us, but people still come here every day seeking their dreams.

Great events make the city a great place to play – Whether you're talking about the world famous Calgary Stampede, Folk Fest, the many cultural and community festivals or a Flames, Stamps, Roughnecks or the many other professional or amateur sporting events, Calgary is a great place to have fun.

Great environment – Blue skies, clean and majestic rivers, magnifi-cent parks, and the Rocky Mountains at our door. Calgary is truly one of the environmental wonders of the world.

Dinosaur Farts and Other Kleinisms

"He can present his arguments, a left wing argument, and that is that everyone should have an equal salary, now matter how hard they work…that salary should all go back to the government, and that should be distributed equally. Well, you know what they used to call that and maybe they still do — it's communism."

- Edmonton Journal, February 1, 1997

"Why do Liberals exist? To get me fired, and they will use every dirty, rotten, slimy, under-the-earth means to do that."

- Edmonton Journal, November 5, 1997

"Because I'm a man of my words, I like to keep my promises and I do have fun believe it or not, some days, most days … (but after 13 years in the job) … well, the joy is looking forward to retirement."

- Edmonton Journal, December 21, 2005

"You would have to eat 10 billion meals of brains, spinal cords, ganglia, eyeballs and tonsils to get the disease."

-Klein on the chances of being infected by mad cow disease

"You get a lot of free dinners but after that you get sort of tired, especially when you quit drinking, and then it's no fun at all, so I don't know why they would want to do it."

- Klein talking to reporters at the Calgary Stampede on July 10, 2006 about his potential successors.

"I'm no doctor, but I think that Mr. McGuinty's got a case of premature speculation."

- Klein in March 2006, commenting on Ontario Premier Dalton McGuinty's declaration that Ontario would oppose any America-style health reforms that might lead to two-tiered care.

"We're basically the same party, you know. Conservatives and Republicans are quite the same."

- Klein speaking to reporters in Washington after a 2003 meeting with U.S. Vice President Dick Cheney.

"I guess any self-respecting rancher would have shot, shoveled and shut up, but he didn't do that."

- Klein's 2003 advice to an Alberta farmer on what he should have done after finding a BSE-infected cow in his herd.

"Dinosaur farts."

**- Klein's 2002 offering on what might have brought
on the Ice Age that killed off dinosaurs.**

THE TALE OF KING RALPH

Both Liberal and Conservative parties in Canada came courting the
very popular of Alberta's biggest city. As he showed throughout his
political career, Klein had a very keen sense of the political winds. In
1988, he supported Conservative Brian Mulroney in the federal election. The following year he ran as a Conservative in the provincial
election, winning a seat as the representative for the Elbow Park riding in Calgary.

He was appointed minister of the environment by then premier
Don Getty and fueled controversy when he flipped off a protester of
the Oldman river dam project. He very quickly became the heir
apparent, and won the party leadership in 1992.

He led the Conservatives to victory in 1993, garnering 51 of 83
seats and nearly 45 percent of the popular vote. He rode to another
victory in 1997 with 51 percent of the popular vote. Then in 2001 he
won an unprecedented 62 per cent of the popular vote, with the
Conservatives sweeping 74 of 83 seats. It has been argued that a
chimp could govern Alberta, but Klein is not given enough credit for
his fiscal prudence in managing a burgeoning treasury.

His colourful remarks ensured that he would be squarely in the
media spotlight for most of his career. From having a pie smashed
into his face at a pancake breakfast in Calgary to disparaging
remarks made to homeless people in Edmonton, the media often had
a field day with his antics.

While many elected officials across Canada refer to their time in
office as terms, Ralph Klein's 14 year run as premier is widely referred
to as the reign of King Ralph. It has been a colourful, albeit uneven
run. He has legitimately become a national figure, an unusual feat for a
provincial politician. Albertans and Calgarians will miss the controversy
and unrehearsed candor that characterized his premiership.

They Said It

PROVINCIAL AND FEDERAL REPRESENTATION

- Provincial Legislature: 23 of 83 seats
- Canada House of Commons: 21 of 308 seats
- Senate of Canada: 6 of 100 seats

Source: Elections Alberta; Alberta Government.

WOMEN AND CALGARY POLITICS

Women were first granted the right to vote in municipal elections in 1894. It would be more than two decades later however, in 1916, that Alberta became the third in Canada to extend the provincial vote to women.

- in 1917, Annie Gale became Calgary's first female alderman, as well as the first female to serve on any municipal council in the entire British empire.
- today, five of the city's 14 aldermen are women.

Did you know...

that with just over seven months under his belt, Donald Hartman was Calgary's shortest serving mayor? He was appointed mayor in March 1989 on 'King Ralph's' departure for the provincial legislature and remained in office until regular elections the following October.

They Said It

> "If women had the vote there would be no need to come twice asking for better legislation for women and children, no need to come again and again for the appointment of women inspectors where women and children are employed; we would not ask in vain for the raising of the wage or consent. We do not want to vote as men, we want to vote as women—the more womanly the better."
>
> **– Suffragist Henrietta Muir Edwards, 1907**

THE POWER OF A WOMAN

With the wide range political influences and ideas swirling in and out of Calgary around the turn of the century, it's no wonder the place was a source of energy for women and their political struggles. One of the city's most notable ladies was teacher Maude Riley.

Her first great achievement came in 1913, when she was able to persuade the local police force to hire female matrons. She was instrumental in the 1918 startup of the Calgary Child Welfare Society, an organization that would become the Alberta Council on Child and Family Welfare five years later. Keen was president of the Council from its inception in 1923 to 1962.

She also played a major role in getting Alberta's family courts up and running and was an important figure the Council on Child Welfare and the Foothills Provincial General Hospital Board.

She also sat on the executive committee of the Alberta Federation of Women, toiled for several years with the Calgary Local Council of Women and worked closely with Henrietta Edwards – of the Famous Five ladies – on the Provincial Executive of the National Council of Women.

Did you know...

that the Reform Party was formed by Preston Manning in Calgary in 1987?

THE PRIME MINISTER CONNECTION

- In 1930, New Brunswick-born Richard Bedford Bennett was the first Prime Minister to be elected from a Calgary riding.
- In 1979, High River native Joe Clark - elected in Calgary South - became Canada's youngest Prime Minister, a position he held for seven months before his minority government fell.
- In 2006, Stephen Harper and his new Conservatives won a minority government, sending the Calgary Southwest representative to the top of Parliament Hill.

Did you know...

that City Aldermen first earned a salary for their duties in 1935?

Weblinks

Calgary's Municipal Government
www.calgary.ca
Everything you want to know about the Mayor, Aldermen and City politics is available at this web locale.

Premier Ed Stelmach
www.premier.alberta.ca
Visit the premier's website for Premier Stelmach biography, and takes of the latest issues and more.

Found Locally: Calgary
www.foundlocally.com/Calgary/Local/Government.htm
This website offers information about Calgary's politics and political representation at all levels of government.

Then and Now

Present day Calgary sits on land that has for 11,000 years been the domain of the Blackfoot people. It wasn't until 1873 that John Glenn, an Irish veteran of the American Civil war, became Calgary's first documented European settler.

Glenn and his new wife, Adelaide, a Métis from Lac Ste. Anne, packed all their worldly possessions onto the back of a single mule and made the difficult journey to establish in present day Calgary. Impressed by the fertile valley of Fish Creek and Bow River, the Glenns built their first home.

Not long after the Glenns arrived, the site became a post for the North West Mounted Police and was named Fort Calgary. With the arrival of the Canadian Pacific Railway (CPR) in 1883, Calgary experienced its first boom, exploding into an important commercial, ranching and agricultural centre. In 1884, just a decade after the Glenns first settled, Calgary was incorporated as a town, and by 1894 as a city.

Although oil was first discovered in Alberta in 1902, it wasn't until the 1950s that it had an impact on the economy. In the first half of the last century, the city was first a ranching, then an agricultural and transportation center.

The discovery of huge oil reserves at Leduc in 1947 changed Calgary forever. The city had always attracted the ambitious and those looking for a new beginning. This time the city attracted them in even greater numbers. The population mushroomed from 403,000 in 1971, to 657,000 in 1988, to more than one million today. In spite of the success of modern Calgary, the city with the fastest growing economy in Canada, "Cow Town" remains proudly rooted in its traditional culture of its First People, hotel saloons, cowboy bars and hockey.

Calgarians old and new will tell you it is a great place to live, work and play. More than 130 years after the Glenn family established their home in the area, people from across Canada and, indeed, the world, continue to see Calgary as land of hope and opportunity; a city where one can imagine new possibilities, realize dreams and build successful futures.

POPULATION, THEN AND NOW

1881:	75
1891:	3,876
1901:	4,091
1911:	43,704
1921:	63,305
1931:	83,761
1941:	88,904
1951:	129,060
1961:	249,641
1971:	403,319
1981:	591,857
1991:	636,104
2001:	1,043,000
2006:	1,079,310

GENDER (IM)BALANCE

Number of Males per 1,000 Females in Calgary, 1891-1971

1891:	1247.0
1901:	1246.5
1911:	1550.0

1921:	1010.0
1931:	1072.5
1941:	1004.1
1951:	983.1
1961:	1007.7
1971:	993.0

Source: University of Calgary.

Bio FATHER ALBERT LACOMBE

Father Albert Lacombe was a Roman Catholic Missionary who figured prominently in early Calgary history. Although Lacombe was a man of his time and was committed to assimilating Canada's First People, the Metis, Plains Cree and Blackfoot (now Siskika) recognized in Lacombe a sincere wish to help their people. In fact, the Blackfoot dubbed him Aahsosskitsipahpiwa, "the man of the good heart" and the Cree knew him as Kamiyoatchakwêt, "the noble soul." Lacombe was equally well-regarded by non-Natives. In 1883, when the first train arrived in Calgary, Father Lacombe was invited to a prestigious private luncheon with Canadian Pacific Railway (CPR) brass to thank him for his diplomatic efforts at stemming a feared Native uprising against the railway. CPR President George Stephen was so grateful for Lacombe's negotiation skills that he resigned from his post for an hour, instating Lacombe in his stead. Father Lacombe returned the favour by appointing Smith the pastor of St. Mary's parish, also for one hour. Lacombe is remembered for saying his heart would always remain in the Rocky Mountain foothills. When he died in 1916, his body was carried by CPR train to St. Albert where he was buried in Cree territory. The Sisters of Mercy took his remark about the foothills literally and they preserved his heart there for nearly 75 years, displaying it on the mantel in the chapel of Lacombe's former home. They eventually laid it to rest in 1992, appropriately enough, in Blackfoot country. The tombstone reads: "Here rests his heart."

ETHNIC ORIGINS OF CALGARY'S POPULATION

Ethnic Group	1901	1961
Asian	64	2,688
British	3,578	147,030
French	125	9,528
German	197	26,917
Italian	0	4,720
Dutch	23	8,682
Scandinavian	195	4,493
Russian	64	3,584
Ukrainian	0	7,075
Polish	0	5,106
Jewish	0	1,856
Aboriginal	101	335
Others	51	27,627

Source: University of Calgary

ON THE RANGE

After 1867, as the new nation of Canada continued its westward expansion, it envisioned an agrarian west. In 1872, the Canadian government passed the Dominion's Land Act. Although the plan was to attract farmers, initial planting efforts met with little success. Newcomers, however, quickly realized that while southern Alberta might pose problems to the farmer, its snow-sapping Chinooks, sheltering coulees and quenching mountain streams made it prime ranching territory.

The government of Canada welcomed the ranchers, initiating a long-lease system that allowed ranchers to lease up to 100,000 acres for twenty-one years at a paltry cost of one cent, per acre, per year. This incentive attracted large, for-profit ranching companies which quickly

Did you know...

that archeologists have found evidence of bison hunts that took place as far back as 8,000 years ago along what is now 17th Ave?

dominated the ranching industry around Calgary. Ranching became the financial backbone of southern Alberta and the wealthy cattlemen part of the area's political and social scenes.

CONNECTED TO THE LAND

Encouraged by the Minister of Immigration, Clifford Sifton, and buoyed by the European demand for wheat, thousands of immigrants moved to southern Alberta to try their hands at farming in the late

Bio NORM KWONG

Born Lim Kwong Yew in 1929, Kwong joined the Calgary Stampeders in 1948 after a successful high school football career. With the handle of "The China Clipper," the 5'7" 170 lb fullback ran over opposing defenses and in the process set 30 league records, earning the recognition as "All-Canadian Fullback."

Not all those records were with the Stampeders though, as he did join the hated Edmonton Eskimos in 1951. In all, he helped Alberta teams win four Grey Cups, and when he retired from the game in 1960, he had amassed an incredible 9,022 rushing yards. He was named to the Canadian Football League's Hall of Fame in 1969 and the Canadian Sports Hall of Fame in 1975.

After retirement, Kwong settled into a successful real estate career in Calgary and in 1980 was a key member of the group of local businessmen who brought then Atlanta Flames franchise of the NHL to Calgary. When the Calgary Flames won the NHL championship in 1989, Kwong became one of the few Canadians that could boast having their names on both the Grey Cup and Stanley Cup.

Still in sports, from 1988-1991 Kwong was also the president of the Calgary Stampeders, and many still credit him for saving the franchise from financial problems and in doing so, likely saving the CFL as well.

In recognition of his work on behalf of multiculturalism, his commitment to his communities, and his accomplishments in sports and business, Kwong was named to the Order of Canada in 1998. In January 2005, Prime Minister Paul Martin named Kwong Alberta's Lieutenant Governor.

They Said It

19th century. As they did, the economy and politics of the Calgary region shifted and the town became the centre of a western wheat and farm equipment trade.

Although lucrative, farming had attendant risks. Growing conditions and wheat prices proved unstable, and success one year could melt into dismal failure the next. Railroad tariffs also proved to be the bane of the existence of Alberta wheat farmers. Determined to fight what they saw as railroad exploitation in 1906, farmers banded together to form the United Farmers of Alberta, a movement so powerful it was, for a time in the 1920s, the government of the province.

Although oil would eclipse agriculture as the source of Calgary's wealth in the 20th century, Calgary's political, economic and cultural heritage is one very much wedded to the soil.

EXPANSION OF ALBERTA'S OIL AND GAS ECONOMY

Year	Wells	Barrels (Millions)	Exploration Expenditure ($ millions)
1947	502	6.3	25
1960	9,878	133.5	353
1972	14,168	522.2	870

Source: Foran's. Frontier Metropolis

Did you know...

that prior to the arrival of the Europeans in the Rocky Mountain foothills, the Tsuu T'ina (Sarcee) dubbed the area of modern Calgary "Kootisaw," which means "meeting of the waters"?

Tumultuous Times in Turner Valley

In 1888, ranchers Sam Howe and John Ware observed a curious sight in a field near Calgary — oil floating on a pool of standing water. By 1911, such sights were common. Ontarian William Herron was intrigued. That year, Herron purchased farmland and by the beginning of January 1913, he and his partner, Archibald W. Dingman, had established Calgary Petroleum Products and were digging for oil. In August 1913, drilling began at the Dingman No. 1 site. On May 14th, 1914, it struck black gold.

News of the discovery spread like a prairie wildfire. Seemingly overnight, 500 speculating companies sprung up in Calgary. Although westerners were interested, easterners with deep pockets were not. Without eastern capital, further oil exploration was not possible. When World War I broke out, the nation's attention turned elsewhere and the Turner Valley oil exploits fizzled.

In the 1920s, oil companies, lacking a market for their product, simply burned excess oil and fiery Turner Valley became known as "Hell's Half Acre."

As fate would have it, it was also at this time that Turner Valley got its second wind. A Quebec engineer, Robert Brown, was convinced that profitable petroleum lurked below the surface, and in 1934, Brown's Turner Valley Royalties Company drilled deeper than ever and found what they were looking for.

In 1936 the company's No. 1 well ushered in Turner Valley's golden age. By the end of the '30s, Turner Valley boasted 70 wells and an annual revenue of $10 million. Turner Valley would remain the heart of Alberta's petroleum industry until the 1940s when the field began to decline and the oil strike at Leduc drew oil moguls' attention northward.

They Said It

RAILWAY

From the time of Confederation, the westward expansion of a railroad was part of Canada's plan for the west. In August 1883, young Fort Calgary was just a stagecoach pit stop between Edmonton and Fort Benton, Montana. The previous year, however, Ottawa had come up with a plan to extend the Canadian Pacific Railway over a southern route through the Rockies, and the modest Fort Calgary was slated to become the hub of this massive undertaking.

- August 11, 1883: Crowds cheer as the first supply train arrives.
- July 1, 1886: The Pacific Express (the CPR's first transcontinental train) pulls into Calgary.
- July 21, 1890: 2,500 Calgarian residents look on as construction begins on the Calgary and Edmonton railway line.
- July 27, 1891: The C & E is complete.
- 1903: The CPR takes over the C & E.
- January 1990: Crowds gather to unsuccessfully protest the last run of the Canadian, VIA Rail's TransCanada passenger route.

Did you know...

that the Calgary Flames were purchased from Atlanta in 1982 for $16 million?

Did you know...

that Calgarian Bruno Scherzinger brought the world the bowling alley pin-resetting machine when he patented it in 1956?

TRANSIT

In the early 20th century, Calgarians toyed with the idea of a communi-ty "transit" in the form of a horse drawn caravan and an early bus serv-ice that rolled over unpaved roads. In 1907, these plans came to fruition when residents voted to borrow money to construct a street railway.

In July 1909, the first streetcar of the Calgary Municipal Railway made its inaugural run from downtown to Victoria park, with 16 miles of track and 12 electric street cars. By the end of its first week, more than 35,000 people had paid the nickle fare.

Bio GUY WEADICK

Born in Rochester, New York on February 23, 1885, wrangler Guy Weadick had a life-long fascination with trick roping. Legend has it that after seeing his first wild west show he resolved to become a ranch hand and cowboy. His first chance came in the form of a way-ward dairy cow in a Winnipeg back alley. As his three cousins looked on, young Guy reined in the escaped bovine.

Years later, he would realize his dream by landing a job as a trick roper with the Buffalo Bill's Wild West show. After visiting Calgary on tour, Weadick couldn't shake the idea of a large scale spectacle cel-ebrating the rich history of the cowboy way, and he approached four ranchers — Pat Burns, A.E. Cross, George Lane and Archie McLean — with his idea. They shared Weadick's vision and each anted up $25,000 to fund the event.

The first Calgary Exhibition and Stampede was held in July 1912, and was a monumental success. The population of Calgary doubles for ten days with visitors coming from across the prairies and the United States to take in the rodeo, parade and agriculture fair.

Weadick's contribution to the prosperity and identity of Calgary continues to be recognized. The Calgary Exhibition and Stampede has named an award in his memory, bestowing it to one exceptional chuck-wagon or rodeo rider who best represents the spirit of the west.

CARS

On July 3,1901, W.F. Cochrane introduced the automobile to Calgary. His car, a steam-powered Locomobile, was a strange looking contraption. Steered by a tiller and sporting a wicker basket, few thought that autos would become permanent fixtures on Calgary streets.

Five years later, their future seemed far more secure. On March 4th, 1906, Calgary Mayor H.W. White, completed the first car trip from Edmonton to Calgary. White's Ford left Edmonton early Saturday morning. Navigating snow-covered roads, the going was slow. White arrived in Calgary at 7pm on Sunday.

A month later, in response to the growing number of cars on Alberta roadways, a provincial MLA introduced a motion to limit car speeds. A limit of 20 mph was applied in the country and 10 mph in city limits. The law stipulated that if a car encountered a horse, the car had to come to a full stop to allow the horse to pass and also required all cars to be registered.

In 1921, the city of Calgary introduced its first parking ticket and by 1924, cars in the city of Calgary could fuel up at one of 61 "filling stations" in the city.

The first automatic traffic signals in the city were installed at the intersections created by 7th and 8th Avenues S and Centre Street and 1st Street W. By the late 1950s, the city could boast 115 automatic signals that provided safer, more organized roadways, as did a switch to the one-way system for downtown roads in 1965.

Source: Glenbow Museum; Calgary Police Service; City of Calgary.

PLANES, PAST AND PRESENT

It was during the first year of World War I that Calgary joined the world's aviation ranks, opening the door of its first hangar in Bowness, about 10 km outside

Did you know...

Calgary's first recorded fire took place in 1885, causing bystanders to throw snowballs?

of town. Between then and the start of WWII, two additional sites opened to transport people to and from the city by plane.

- In 1939, Calgary's airport first opened where it stands today.
- Ottawa took it over one year later to serve the WWII effort.
- When the keys were handed back to Calgary in 1949, the airport boasted four runways and five hangars.

Albert and Vera Dick:
Calgary's Titanic Survivors

By the early 20th century, Albert Adrian Dick was a successful Calgary businessman, co-owner of the famous Hotel Alexandra on 9th Ave. S.E.

In the early spring of 1911, Dick and his seventeen-year-old bride, Vera, left for their honeymoon tour of the Holy Land and Europe.

The newlyweds' journey home was to be a leisurely one — they had booked first class passage on the world-famous Titanic. The couple was enamoured of the sea, and Vera later recalled that "even in Canada where we have clear nights I have never seen such a clear sky or stars so bright."

The Dick's honeymoon holiday was, however, to become a nightmare. On the evening of April 15th, 1912, the newlyweds were sleeping peacefully when the doomed ship hit the iceberg. The couple did not hear or feel a thing. Only when a steward knocked on their door did the young couple learn of the accident and were instructed to don life jackets. Being among the fortunate, the Dicks were escorted to a life raft and survived.

Life after the disaster was difficult. Albert was widely criticized for surviving the disaster, and rumours circulated that he had dressed as a woman to escape the sinking ship. His business suffered as a result and he was compelled to sell his hotel. Albert Dick nevertheless remained active in Calgary's real estate industry and Vera became a well-known vocalist.

Did you know...

- In 1956, the new terminal (considered Canada's most modern) opened only to be obsolete within a decade thanks to the arrival of the jet age.
- Calgary sold the airport to Ottawa for $2 million and a promise to build a swanky new building and upgrade the entire airport in 1966.
- The Calgary International Airport — up until then called McCall Field — was born in 1977. Today, this state-of-the-art aviation complex covers nearly 21 km^2, offers .5 km^2 in parking and paved roads, boasts 1.89 km^2 of airfield taxi and runways, offers 0.12 km^2 of terminal space and pumps 1.5 million litres of aircraft fuel each day.

Source: Calgary International Airport.

DROUGHT OF EPIC PROPORTIONS

On Black Tuesday, October 29th, 1929, the crash of North American stock markets ushered in one of the worst recessions in Canadian history.

Nowhere in Canada was harder hit than the prairies, where economic devastation was accentuated by ecological crisis: drought. The decade of the 1930s not only saw bank accounts dry up but also the land itself.

Unable to grow crops, 47,000 farm dwellers were driven off the land and nearly 9,000 farms were abandoned between 1931 and 1936 alone.

This century, fears have renewed that history may be repeating itself. Drought struck the prairies again in 2001 and 2002.

Did you know...

Did you know...

that in 1921, a Calgary hen earned a world record when she laid a record-setting egg? Weighing more than 5 ounces, the enormous egg measured 8 inches in circumference around the tips.

THE GREAT DEPRESSION

At the depths of the depression, one-fifth of Calgary's 75,000 people were out of work and compelled to rely on relief. A family of five had to live on $60/month.

LET THERE BE LIGHT

In 1889, the Calgary Electric Lighting Company (Calgary Electric) and the Calgary Water Power Company Limited were contracted by the city to provide streetlights. In light of such stiff competition, in 1894, Calgary Electric closed while the Water Company continued to serve the city. In 1904, the city constructed its own electric light plant, which opened the following year. Only in 1928 did the city start buying its electricity.

Weblinks

The Glenbow Museum

www.glenbow.org

Click your way around an impressive collection of historical archives with such novelties as prairie songwriters' sheet music and photographs from Calgary's earliest settlers. Current exhibitions are also showcased, along with donor lists and school programs.

Our Future/Our Past

www.albertaheritage.net/directory/digitization_project.html

Interested in learning more about the city's history? Visit this site, a project of the Heritage Community Foundation.

The First People

The grasslands and prairies surrounding Calgary's modern day sky-scrapers are the traditional lands of the Blackfoot Nation and the Tsuu T'ina (Sarcee) who have lived and hunted in the region for more than 10,000 years.

The Blackfoot Nation was made of three distinct bands, the Siksika (Blackfoot), the Kainai (Blood), and the Piikani (Peigan). All spoke the same Algonquin language, and were allies against common enemies such as the Cree.

The Tsuu T'ina spoke an Athapaskan language and had different customs than the Blackfoot, issues which caused periodic dissent between the two.

ABORIGINAL PEOPLE IN CALGARY
- Total Aboriginal population: 19,760
- Number of men: 9,355
- Number of women: 10,405

MEDIAN AGE
- Total: 25.9
- Men: 25.1
- Women: 26.7

ON THE RISE

The Aboriginal population of Calgary is the fastest growing of any urban centre in Canada, increasing 10.5 percent between 1996 and 2001. Three-quarters of the rise came from immigration — 45 percent from elsewhere in Canada, 35 percent from the rest of Alberta.

In addition to the 21,910 Aboriginal residents in Calgary (2001 census), another 32,000 Aboriginal people live within a 2.5-hour drive of Calgary. If Calgary's Aboriginal population continues to grow at the rate that it did between 1996 and 2001 (44 percent over five years), there will be an Aboriginal population of 65,000 people in Calgary by 2017.

The Aboriginal population in Calgary is about evenly split between First Nations and Metis, with a pinch of Inuit to spice things up.

Source: Statistics Canada.

EDUCATION AND EMPLOYMENT

Calgary's Aboriginal population is the most highly educated, internet-connected in Alberta, boasting a solid 34 percent of the population 25 or older with a trade, college or university certificate or diploma.

Calgary leads Alberta in Aboriginal self-employment, and run 18 percent of the province's Aboriginal-owned businesses (not bad for having just 14 percent of the Aboriginal population).

Source: Calgary Urban Aboriginal Initiative.

INCOMES OF CALGARY'S ABORIGINAL PEOPLE
- Average annual earnings: $24,282
- Median total income: $17,770
- Median household income: $46,620

UNEMPLOYMENT RATES (PERCENT)
- Total: 10.1
- Men: 9.8
- Women: 10.5

NUMBER OF ABORIGINAL DWELLINGS IN CALGARY

- Total: 9,425
- Owned dwellings: 4,070
- Rented dwellings: 5,355

ABORIGINAL LANGUAGES

- Percentage of Aboriginal people in Calgary whose first language learned and understood is Aboriginal: 4.1
- Percentage who regularly speak an Aboriginal language at home: 2.5
- Percentage with a knowledge of an Aboriginal language: 5.8

Source: Statistics Canada.

OLD MAN CREATION STORY

The Blood and the Blackfoot share a creation myth of Napioa, or Napi, Old Man. The story begins with a world that was covered in water. Old Man sent various animals to see what was below all the water. Only a muskrat returned with something of this underwater world, and he was bearing a ball of mud.

Using this mud, Old Man shaped the earth, animals and plants. Then he made the first people and the bison and taught the people how to hunt them. Once Old Man felt his work was complete, he climbed up a mountain peak and disappeared, promising to return someday.

WANNABE

Chief Buffalo Child Long Lance, a celebrated author and legendary ladies man who wrote about the Plains Indians for the *Calgary Herald* in the late 1920s, was born Sylvester Long in North Carolina. The faker parlayed a Blackfoot friend's life into a best-selling "autobiography," and nabbed a role in Hollywood before a real Aboriginal co-star spilled the beans, leaving Lance to slink off in disgrace.

Bio BLACKFOOT CHIEF CROWFOOT: WARRIOR, ORATOR, DIPLOMAT

Of all the warriors and diplomats of his time, Isapo-Muxiha, better known as Crowfoot, was one of the most influential, making peace between various First Nations groups and becoming a guiding force in the negotiation of Treaty 7. Isapo-Muxiha believed that the relentless incursion of Europeans into Aboriginal lands demanded conciliation and cooperation not only among his own Blood people and other First Nations of the southern Albertan plains, but also with Europeans. This would be his life mission.

Crowfoot was born into the Blood Tribe of the Blackfoot Confederacy in about 1830. As a teenager, in the custom of his people, Crowfoot accompanied older men on an enemy raid. When he was wounded in battle, he earned his name Isapo-Muxika, after a relative killed several years before.

Crowfoot demonstrated his leadership and warrior abilities at a young age. By the age of 20, he had been involved in 19 battles. As a grown man, he rarely went to war, choosing instead to raise horses and lend his leadership to tribal affairs. In 1865, he became Minor Chief. At about the same time, Crowfoot came to the attention of the white population when he and his men fought off a band of Cree who threatened Europeans' presence on the prairies. Thereafter, Crowfoot had the friendship of non-Native traders and missionaries. By the early 1870s, Crowfoot's status as Minor Chief gave way to a more vaunted position in his community.

In 1873, a Blood raid on a Cree camp cost Crowfoot his eldest son. Some time later, he met a young Cree man who bore a striking resemblance to his beloved son. In Blackfoot custom, Crowfoot adopted the young man — a man named Poundmaker. Poundmaker returned to his own people where he himself became an important chief. The bond between Crowfoot and Poundmaker would positively influence oft-stormy Cree-Blackfoot relations.

Crowfoot encouraged peaceable relations with Europeans as well. It was thanks to his friendship with officials of the North West Mounted Police that European settlement in Blackfoot territory occurred in relative peace. Indeed, in 1877, Crowfoot became a lead negotiator of Treaty 7 — an agreement he believed would create the basis for harmony in the prairie west. Aboriginal signatories selected Crowfoot to respond to the negotiations on their behalf.

Crowfoot signed the treaty in optimism. His optimism, however, soon gave way to despair and anger. As bison disappeared from the prairies, the federal Department of Indian Affairs displayed a shocking lack of concern for the plight of starving Aboriginals. By the mid 1850s, the second Riel uprising was mounting and Crowfoot was torn. While he sympathized with his adopted son's people, the Cree — some of whom sided with Riel — and while he had lost much faith in the government, Crowfoot continued to believe that peace was imperative and he refused to take up arms against the government.

The English press glorified Crowfoot for his pro-government stance, but Crowfoot, increasingly disillusioned with Ottawa's failure to live up to its treaty promises, was probably plagued by doubt over his decision.

His last years of life were difficult ones. Personal tragedy beset the Chief. He suffered through ill-health and blindness and endured the deaths of many of his children. A final blow came when his adoptive son, Poundmaker, was imprisoned for his alleged role in the 1885 uprising. Crowfoot managed to win Poundmaker's release, but the Cree Chief died shortly after while visiting Crowfoot's camp. In the spring of 1890, Crowfoot followed Poundmaker to the grave.

They Said It

"My family came from a long line of leaders on both sides. We were taught that there would always be opposition, but not to let others discourage us."

– Artist Joane Cardinal-Schubert

BLACKFOOT SPIRITUALITY AND THE EARTH

The term "ksa'a'hko," literally translated to mean "touching the earth with the feet," is the Blackfoot word for earth. The Earth has a prominent place in Blackfoot spirituality, which has a deep reverence and respect for Mother Earth. This is reflected in the Blackfoot practice of referring to the land, water, plants, animals and their fellow human beings as "all my relations." Everything made by the Creator — rocks, birds, sun, wind and waters — possess spirits.

According to the Blackfoot, the Creator gave them their own territory and the responsibility to care for the land and all their relations, for all time. They are responsible for protecting the land — their inheritance — for future generations.

BISON

The Blackfoot consider the bison to be sacred. According to Blackfoot tradition, the bison was the first animal given to them by the Creator for food and so it is the totem of the oldest sacred society of the Blackfoot, the Horn Society.

Did you know...

that although the term "buffalo" is used to describe the large mammal that once roamed Alberta, these Albertan creatures are, in fact, bison? Buffalo are native only to Africa and Asia.

Aboriginal-Inspired Place Names

Bow River: The Bow River, which divides Calgary and floods about every century, is the translation of "namokhtai," Blackfoot for "weapons river." Local First Nations called the river that because they made bows from the wood of trees growing along its banks.

Deerfoot Trail: The most famous long distance runner in Western Canada, Deerfoot was the name promoters gave Api-kai-ees (Scabby Dried Meat) a Blackfoot who outran a number of professional runners in Calgary. He couldn't outrun the law, though, and Deerfoot's career ended after he cheated in a fixed race.

Bearspaw Dam: According to legend, Stoney Chief Masgaahsid, or Bearspaw, became a warrior when he avenged his mother's murder by killing a Blood Indian. For years he led his people in battle against neighbouring Blood, Blackfoot and Sarcee tribes, but adopted peaceful ways as an older man, and signed Treaty No. 7 in 1877 on behalf of his band.

Shaganappi Point and Shaganappi Trail: "Shaganappi" means rawhide in Cree, specifically the material used in binding and for repairs. Métis travellers used plenty of shaganappi and groups of travellers were often called a shaganappi party, while their camps were called shaganappi outfits.

Sarcee, Peigan and Blackfoot Trails: All named after tribes in the Blackfoot confederacy (although the Sarcee now are called the Tsuu T'ina Nation). The wandering Blackfoot Trail traces part of the path used by the tribe to haul furs from the southern plains to trading posts in Rocky Mountain House and Edmonton.

Weaselhead Flats: The river valley near the future Glenmore Reservoir was named by a government official, but was the home of Chief Bull Head who lived there for about 50 years. No one lives in the urban park nowadays, although it is known to harbour bears, cougars and other wild animals.

Crowchild Trail: Chief David Crowchild (1899-1982) promoted good will between the Sarcee and the City of Calgary, and was a long-time secretary of the Indian Association of Alberta.

They Said It

MEDICINE WHEELS

Scattered across the Prairies but with most concentrations in Southern Alberta, medicine wheels have baffled archaeologists for decades. Built by laying stones in a circular pattern resembling a wagon wheel, these large formations could reach up to 12 m in diameter.

No one agrees as to what the stone structures' original purpose was, not even the region's Aboriginal people. Clearly, however, these meticulously constructed wheels were important. They may have had to do with Aboriginal healing, used to strike a balance between good and evil spirits. Others say that they connected the earth to the stars and universe.

THE SACRED PIPE

The Blackfoot employ smoke ceremonies to offer prayers and petitions to the Great Spirit. The pipe itself is symbolic. Its stone bowl symbolizes the earth, the wooden stem, all plant life, and a leather covering securing the parts represents animal life.

The sacred pipe ceremony begins with the heating of a stone upon which sweet grass, sage or tobacco is sprinkled to generate an aromatic smoke.

The person conducting the smoking ceremony then draws on the pipe, and as he does, offers prayers to the sun, the generator of all life, and to the four directions. The East is the place where people look for light and beginnings, the West symbolizes life's transitions, the North represents the source of cold winds and reflects the purification that comes through struggle and the South, the source of warmth, symbolizes the hope of human aspiration.

Source: Indian and Northern Affairs Canada.

THE BLACKFOOT CONFEDERACY

The Blackfoot Confederacy is made up of five separate bands; the Siksika, Blood, Peigan, Tsuu T'ina and the Gros Ventre of Montana. Together, they refer to themselves as the "Niitsitapii," the real people.

Existing as politically distinct nations, the members of the confederacy occupy well-defined territories and are economically self-sufficient. Each member's nation is politically independent — laws and

Treaty 7

By the 1870s, the First People of the Plains were in dire straights. Overwhelmed by an increasing number of settlers and starving as the result of the unfathomable demise of the bison, the First People of southern Alberta recognized that their futures demanded reconciliation with the settlers and the Canadian government.

And so, in September 1877, representatives of Canada, Britain, the Siksika (Blackfoot), the Kainai (Blood), the Piikani (Peigan), the Tsuu T'ina (Sarcee) and the Nakoda (Stoney), gathered to sign the seventh of eleven numbered treaties negotiated between Canada and the First People.

The letter of the treaty guaranteed each member five dollars a year, one square mile of land per five people, schools, hunting and fishing supplies, and protection of subsistence rights. The spirit of the Treaty, however, remains a subject of discord.

For the First People, Treaty 7 is a treaty of peace, a sacred agreement that spells out how the First People will share the land with newcomers or how they will stop encroachment where negotiations with newcomers fail. They do not believe they ceded land. To government officials, however, the treaty was a means to a final end — a practical solution that wrestled western lands from the hands of First Nations. It is an agreement that confined the First People to reserves thus allowing the westward railway to be built and European settlements to be established on the prairies.

This ideological divide is one that exists to this day, and the real meaning of Treaty 7 is still very hotly debated.

protocols do not allow interference in one another's internal affairs except by invitation.

SOCIAL ORGANIZATION

Dependent as they were on bison, the Blackfoot and Tsuu T'ina spent the seasons following the bison and other animals upon which they depended. In the winter, they lived in small groups along rivers — close enough to the bison but near enough to other groups to offer mutual protection. In the summer, larger groups assembled in camps on the plains.

The plains people lived in bands shaped by residential groups, rather than by family ties. These groups, or bands, were flexible, and people could easily move between them, and in times of strife, join together in defense.

Polygamy was accepted and seen as the right thing to do to protect widowed women. Divorce was also permitted and could be initiated by either the wife or husband.

THE NAMES OF THE FIRST PEOPLE

The three nations of the Blackfoot speak Algonquin-based languages, while the Tsuu T'ina speak Athapaskan.
- The Blackfoot call themselves "Soyitapi" — prairie people.
- Piikani is the name of the Peigan. According to Blackfoot legend, a traveler called them Apikuni, or scabby hides, because they wore robes that still had meat and hair clinging to them.
- Kainai is the name of the Blood, meaning many chiefs. As the story goes, the same traveler who visited the Peigan wanted to meet the chief. Everyone he met, however, claimed the title and so he called this group Blackfoot Akainai, or many chiefs.
- Siksika is the name of the Blackfoot. Oral tradition says that the Blood noticed the traveler's moccasins were stained by campfire ash, and called him Blackfoot.
- The name Saxsiiwak which evolved into Sarcee (the Tsuu T'ina) means "strong people" in Athapaskan.

Bio JOANE CARDINAL-SCHUBERT: ABORIGINAL ARTIST

Artist Joane Cardinal-Schubert has challenged Canadians to rethink Aboriginal art. Cardinal-Schubert's innovative use of colour and her images of tepees, human shapes and animal forms, such as horses, bears and buffalo, create images that are at once rooted in her Aboriginal heritage, and also the product of "western" materials and techniques.

The themes of her work in many ways reflect the ongoing efforts of Aboriginal people to have their cultures acknowledged, their rights recognized and past injustices redressed.

Joane Cardinal-Schubert was born in Red Deer in 1942, the oldest girl in a large family which includes her brother, famed architect Douglas Cardinal. Her encouraging parents nourished both her creativity and her pride in her Blackfoot heritage.

In 1977, she graduated with a Fine Arts degree from the University of Calgary. Before long, Cardinal-Schubert was making a mark on Canada's art scene. One of Canada's most renowned artists, in 1986 she was invited to join the esteemed Royal Canadian Academy of the Arts. Exhibits of her work have graced walls of galleries around the world.

In 1999, a retrospective of her work titled "Two Decades," opened at the Muttart Gallery in Calgary. Her work has been awarded countless accolades such as the Commemorative Medal of Canada in 1993, the Queen's Golden Jubilee Medal in 2002, and in 2003 Cardinal-Schubert was awarded an Honorary Doctor of Laws degree from her alma mater, the University of Calgary.

Cardinal-Schubert has creative talent that extends far beyond the canvass. In addition to writing — pieces of which have been published internationally in art magazines, catalogues and books — she has also worked in theatre, film, and video.

They Said It

STORY ROBES

For centuries before the arrival of Europeans, the Siksika, Blood and Peigan recorded their history on bison hides used for tepee covers and liners or robes. After Europeans and federal Indian agents arrived in the west, these stories were recorded on the pages of Department of Indian Affairs ledger books. These pictorial "stories" commemorated certain events such as battles, a horse raid or some other significant event.

SUNDANCE

The Blackfoot followed the seasons closely, regularly connected with Mother Earth through daily and annual ceremonies. Many of these ceremonies occurred in the summer months, a time of year that brought together large segments of the population.

The Sundance was one such ceremony. It was a time of spiritual renewal and purification and witnessed the fulfillment of spiritual promises for the benefit of a loved one. During the gatherings, the main warrior, religious, women's, children's and police societies held their own ceremonies.

One such ceremony saw men pierce their chests with wooden skewers that were attached by a rope to a centre pole. As they danced

Did you know...

that between 1780 and 1782 thousands of Aboriginal people on the western plains were killed by a smallpox epidemic?

They Said It

"The government put forward its proposals for a future Indian policy a year and a half ago. These stimulated and focused debate and have served a necessary purpose. They are no longer a factor in the debate. The government does not intend to force progress along the directions set out in the proposal of June 1969. The future direction will be that which emerges in meetings between Government and Indian representatives and people."

– 1971, Jean Chrétien's retraction of the very unpopular White Paper

around the pole, the tethered men pulled backwards until the skewers ripped free from their chests. In this way, the men sacrificed themselves to benefit a loved one who was ill.

Gatherings such as the Sundance were also politically important, for it was here that chiefs and other head men would make decisions regarding war and peace with neighbouring groups.

WHITE AND A RED PAPER

The 1960s began with optimism for Natives in Alberta. Across North America, as the civil rights movement gathered steam, their "Red Power" movement asserted Natives' political, territorial and cultural rights, challenged oppressive laws to which they were subject and demanded that the authority of the Canadian Department of Indian Affairs and Northern Development (DIAND) be replaced with self-government and meaningful Native control of Native lands and resources.

It was in this climate that the Liberal government of Pierre Elliott Trudeau decided to overhaul the Indian Act. In 1968, Trudeau's Minister of Indian Affairs, a young Jean Chrétien met with Native communities across Canada, and was advised that Natives were most concerned with land claim and treaty rights recognition and an assurance of Native peoples' special status in Canada.

By June 1969, Ottawa's Indian Act revisions were complete and Native leaders were flown to Ottawa for the new Act's unveiling. On

June 25th, Native leaders listened from the House of Commons Gallery as Chrétien delivered the now infamous White Paper on Indian Policy. Just ten pages long, the White Paper made some stunning recommendations — recommendations that clearly ignored Native wishes. Without addressing the concerns they had raised in consultation, the White Paper called for the Indian Act to be repealed, for treaties to be terminated and for the DIAND to be eliminated.

Native people were outraged and united in their opposition. While Native organizations across the country spoke out against it, it was the Alberta Indian Association (AIA) that penned the official Native response to Ottawa's proposal. Called Citizens Plus, but known as the Red Paper, the AIA opposed every part of the White Paper. The Red Paper insisted that Natives' special status should continue and that rather than abolish the Indian Act, a new one should be written and a new federal agency — one devoted to its moral and legal obligations — be created. The Red Paper insisted that Ottawa recognize treaty and aboriginal rights and above all, insisted that the offensive White Paper not be implemented. Facing such vehement and widespread opposition, the federal government retracted the White Paper in 1971.

NATIONAL ABORIGINAL AWARENESS DAY
Each June 21st, Aborginal people in Calgary join all other Canadians in celebrating National Aboriginal Awareness Day. Initially proclaimed by governor-general Roméo A. LeBlanc, National Aboriginal Awareness Day was first celebrated in 1996.

Did you know...

The First People who first hunted bison in and around what is now Calgary were around for some 12,000 years before the first Europeans "discovered" the area. The Blackfoot, Tsuu T'ina (Sarcee) and Stony First People have all called this region home.

Weblinks

Treaty 7, Past and Present

www.albertasource.ca/treaty7/index.html

For information about Treaty 7, its history and implications, look at this web page, part of the Alberta Online Encyclopedia Project.

Aboriginal Canada Portal (Calgary)

www.aboriginalcanada.gc.ca/acp/site.nsf/en/ao03034.html

Visit this web site for on-line resources and links to services and organizations pertinent to Aboriginal Youth in Calgary.

Glenbow Museum: Niitsitapi: Our Way of Life

www.glenbow.org/blackfoot

This online exhibit of the Glenbow Museum is dedicated to the culture and history of the Blackfoot and is available in three languages: Blackfoot, English and French.

Go Ahead, Take Five More

As you can probably tell, we are partial to things you can count on one hand. This chapter is just more of that. It is designed to be fun, entertainingand insightful, not only in details about the city, but also about the person making the choices. It is a chapter that could have continued beyond the bounds of this book. Calgarians, famous and not so famous, were literally bursting at the seams with opinions about their city.

TAKE 5: JASON SMITH'S TOP FIVE BATTLE OF ALBERTA MOMENTS

It seems that the rivalry between Alberta's largest cities knows no bounds. It is contested on numerous fronts from backrooms, legislative floors and especially from football fields and hockey arenas. Jason Smith may be an Oiler captain but he is a Calgary boy. After stints with the New Jersey Devils and Toronto Maple Leafs, Calgary's Smith was traded in 1999 to the rivals at the north end of Highway 2. Until the Oilers traded him in 2007 he was warrior in many Battles of Alberta. Here are his picks for one of the most hotly contested rivalries in sport.

1. Theoren Fleury's goal celebration against the Edmonton Oilers in the 1991 playoffs.

2. Wayne Gretzky's slapshot over the shoulder of Mike Vernon in the 1988 playoffs.

3. Doug Flutie and the Calgary Stampeders comeback against the Edmonton Eskimos in the 1992 Western Final. Doug Flutie scores from the one-yard line and his shoe goes flying in the air.

4. Edmonton Eskimos Western Final victory over the Calgary Stampeders in Calgary in 1996. The weather was so awful, it had to be -25 with wind down on the field.

5. The Battle of Alberta never ends. Calgary and Edmonton play eight times each season and it's a battle each time.

JOHN GILCHRIST'S TOP FIVE RESTAURANTS FOR A TRULY CALGARY EXPERIENCE

John Gilchrist has reviewed restaurants for CBC Radio in Calgary since 1980 and has written seven national best-selling books on dining in southern Alberta.

1. The Rimrock at the Fairmont Palliser

Since 1914, The Rimrock (or its various early-day iterations) has served kegs of beer, bowls of creamy clam chowder and herds of Alberta beef to visitors and glitterati from around the world. Included on the guest list are the Prince of Wales (the one who became Edward VIII), Prime Minister R.B. Bennett (a regular by the fireplace) and the Stampede's Big Four founders.

2. Rouge

Located in the historic A.E. Cross House – one of the above-mentioned Big Four and founder of Calgary Brewery – Rouge features the contemporary Calgary cuisine of talented Paul Rogalski. And perhaps the best patio in the city.

3. **River Café**

The only building on Prince's Island – not counting the open-air stage – houses River Café. It's an idyllic setting just a short walk from downtown with a seasonal Canadian menu to match.

4. **Silver Inn**

Is there a more Calgarian dish than ginger beef with its tangy-sweet, gingery, beefy taste? Head for the place that started ginger beef's rise to fame in the 1970s – the Silver Inn. Enjoy the rest of the Beijing-style menu too.

5. **Panorama Dining Room**

Elevate your dining to the top of the Calgary Tower for a view of the sun setting over the Rockies. It's breathtaking; almost enough to distract from some fine Canadian cuisine.

One add-on: If there just isn't enough beef in the above restaurants try a burger at Rocky's Burger Bus. Housed in a former Calgary Transit bus and surrounded by prairie grasses, it's an industrial-zone classic. And you'll be entertained by Richardson Ground Squirrels (gophers) in their natural habitat.

TAKE 5: DUFF GIBSON'S FIVE WAYS TO SLOW DOWN AND ENJOY LIFE

At the 2006 Winter Olympics, skeleton athlete Duff Gibson found four perfect lines down the twisting icy track and in the process authored one of the greatest Olympic stories of all time, and finally discovered what it meant to wear gold. After over twenty years of various sports that included rowing, speed skating and bobsleigh, he took up the daredevil sport of skeleton. Just shy of his 40th birthday, and in what would be his final shot at gold, Gibson achieved his life's goal.

1. **Cruising on the Hog.** A great summertime activity is to take a motorcycle ride out to Bragg Creek, park in front of the Powderhorn Saloon and check out all the sweet rides.

2. **Check Out an Amateur Sport.** Every year within the city limits you have the opportunity to see some of the world's best athletes — and a lot of them are Canadian. What I would recommend from my own experience is to get to the Oval to see a World Cup race, or get to C.O.P. to see a World Cup skeleton, bobsled or luge race in the winter or a World Cup mountain bike race in the summer.

3. **Walk the Dog at Carburn Park.** If you have a dog you'll know what I mean when I ask, why do people go to an off-leash area if they don't want other dogs running up and sniffing their dog? There is an obviously different attitude at Carburn. My wife and I have enjoyed some great conversations learning about the less common breeds you have a chance to see there.

4. **Snowboarding at C.O.P.** Winter enthusiasts may scoff at Canada Olympic Park's relatively low vertical but with its many kickers, flat-tops, rails, and the recent addition of a world class half-pipe, there's absolutely everything you would want or need to get the big air.

5. **Dirt biking.** Rates not that high on the 'slow' aspect but rates very high on the 'enjoy life' aspect. There are lots of great cross-country trails outside of Calgary, and within the city you have the Wild Rose Motorcross Park. Get the gear because you will fall.

TAKE 5: REPORTER SEAN MYER'S TOP FIVE WAYS CALGARY KICKS EDMONTON'S BUTT

Calgary Herald reporter Sean Myers may have been raised in the southern Alberta city but was born in Edmonton and has family connections to the provincial capital.

1. In 2004, Calgary Flames fans spontaneously created the Red Mile, a 40,000-strong street party which everyone was invited and which remained a relatively peaceful celebration of the Flames' unexpected

playoff run. Two years later Edmontonians tried to copy the party for the Oilers' post season successes only to have it descend into a level of violence and destruction that embarrassed many of the city's own citizens.

2. The Calgary Stampede is a massive cultural event that transforms the entire city. It's one hell of a bigger annual bash than anything Edmonton's managed to come up with.

3. Calgary has developed several quaint strolls for shopping, eating and nightlife in the city's older communities which all serve as destination spots while Edmonton really only has Whyte Avenue.

4. Several world class ski areas and wilderness park areas beckon at Calgary's doorstep, much more convenient than the three hour-plus drive Edmonton outdoor enthusiasts face to get to Jasper.

5. One word: Chinooks. While Edmonton spends most winters under mounting snowfalls Calgary has an abundance of sunshine and warm weather to break up the doldrums and bemuse meteorologists.

TAKE 5: SUSAN WEATHERBY'S FIVE BEST CALGARY DAYTRIPS

Susan Weatherby is the mother of two young children. As she says, the expertise of mothers is under utilized and under appreciated. What better experts can there be on daytrips than moms, she says. We agree.

1. **Banff:** Located about 45 minutes west of Calgary, Banff is a must-see on any trip to Calgary. The town of Banff is in Canada's oldest national park and is home to the first of several Canadian Pacific Railway luxury resorts. Resembling more a castle than a hotel, the Banff Springs has hosted kings, queens and the world's elite for over century. The town itself is the center of the playground of the Rocky Mountains boasting the best vertical skiing in the world. Banff is still the launching pad for adventurers wishing to conquer the surrounding peaks.

2. **Dinosaur Capital of Canada:** At the heart of South Central Alberta, the Drumheller Valley offers visitors a unique combination of spectacular scenery and interesting things to do. Rolling fields suddenly give way to steep, dry coulees ridged with the strata of hundreds of years of erosion by time, wind and water. Resembling more the Grand Canyon than the prairies, visitors are surprised to find it home to cactus and rattlesnakes. The centre of one of the world's largest dinosaur finds, Drumheller boasts a unique species named for the province. The Albertasaurus is a smaller version of the T-Rex.

3. **Jasper National Park** and The Columbia Ice Fields: Established in 1907 on the eastern slopes of the Rockies, Jasper is part of the UNESCO Canadian Rocky Mountain Parks World Heritage Site. At over 10,800 km2, the park is a living example of a protected mountain ecosystem that allows for visitors to enjoy solitude, wildlife, outdoor recreation and a wide range of learning opportunities. Within the boundaries of Jasper National Park there are also five National Historic Sites.

4. **Cypress Hills:** Located 325 km southeast of Calgary, Cypress Hills appears as a mirage on the prairies, the only part of North America untouched by the ice age. It is one of the most significant areas of ancient human inhabitation in North America, and archaeological digs have turned up artifacts of the Besant, Lake, Oxbow and Bitterroot cultures. Cypress Hills is now a home to recreational enthusiasts as a skiing, fishing, boating, hunting, hiking and a variety of other activities draw people from around the area.

5. **Kananaskis Country:** Over 4000 sq. km's of playground, this provincial park is only a half hour from Calgary. Kananaskis truly offers something for everyone. From fine dinning, deluxe accommodations, golfing on one of Canada's top courses to hiking, fishing, boating, camping, and even 196 sq km's of off road motoring, you'd be hard pressed to get bored in this gem of the Rockies.